HOW TO GET
THE TOP
JOBS
THAT ARE
NEVER
ADVERTISED

WILLET WEEKS

HOW TO GET
THE TOP
JOBS
THAT ARE
NEVER
ADVERTISED

**KOGAN
PAGE**

YOURS TO HAVE AND TO HOLD

BUT NOT TO COPY

Author's note: All first and last names of actual people cited in this book are camouflaged. Their bestowed names always begin with the same letter; eg 'Sam Smallwood'. With the exception, of course, of Willet Weeks.

First published in 1996

Kogan Page Limited
120 Pentonville Road
London N1 9JN

British Library Cataloguing in Publication Data
A CIP record for this book is available from the British Library.
ISBN 0 7494 1946 6

Typeset by Saxon Graphics Ltd, Derby
Printed and bound in Great Britain by Clays Ltd, St Ives plc

Contents

About the Author

After a boyhood in New Jersey, Willet Weeks launched on a career in newspaper, book and magazine publishing, interrupted by four years of wartime service as an officer in the US Navy. Most of his working life was spent with the *New York Herald Tribune*, where he became manager of the worldwide Herald Tribune Syndicate and News Service and, later, publisher of its Paris edition.

At the height of his work in publishing, the *Herald Tribune* in New York ceased publication, forcing him to seek new directions. His explorations led to the discovery of the nascent activity of personal career counselling for managers. Intrigued, he joined, as a consultant, the leading US company in the field and found the human aspects of the work deeply satisfying.

After three years of practice in New York, Willet Weeks opened, in 1972, a successful branch office in London — eventually becoming its chairman and majority owner. He then expanded his consulting services to the Continent, establishing offices in Paris, Geneva and, most recently, Frankfurt.

A little-known activity at the start, executive career consultancy has since spun off certain organizations offering aid to victims of corporate downsizing, a specialization that is today known as 'outplacement'. However, personal counselling for individuals, as practised by Willet Weeks, continues to provide a confidential service for managers who are voluntarily seeking upward mobility.

Willet Weeks is the author of four books dealing with various aspects of executive development.

Preface

WHY THIS BOOK?

Since the publication of my book, *Moving Ahead in Your Career* (Pitman, London, 1994), I have received letters voicing a certain frustration. The following is typical:

> You offer some helpful suggestions about how to set career objectives. Then you launch right into the matter of how to handle job interviews. What most interests me is what happens in between the two phases — in other words, how to make the right contacts in order to have those productive interviews you write about.

I note that such comments often come from managers who have done well in their careers. It is an irony that many upwardly mobile people belong to a kind of underprivileged group when the time comes to 'market' themselves and their professional skills.

Why is this? They have not learned that the job-seeking methods that worked well at the beginning of their professional life no longer get results. With each step upward, the rules of the game change but many people are unaware of what is happening. While the visible side of the job market served them well as juniors, sooner or later they find out the hard way that replying to position-open advertisements becomes less and less productive.

This lack of contact with the realities of a job search is hardly surprising. Such people may have remained in one organization before seeking a change. Or they may have been invited to make one or two moves by an executive search firm or a personal contact. As a result, the very idea of proactively mounting an effective search is outside the scope of their experience. Not only that, but many people find that the thought of 'selling themselves' (as they tend to see it) is off-putting.

The irony of this becomes clear in the light of another kind of profile: that of the person who has been regularly extruded from companies. Through a painful process of trial, error and a lot of practice, this person ultimately masters the ways to make contact with new possibilities. It is no secret, however, that experience can be a very expensive teacher. Errors, lost time, missed opportunities — to say nothing of the pain of repeated rejection — are characteristic of a botched job search.

Let us dispose quickly of what I have called the visible job market. The best figures obtainable indicate that in 1994 only 30 per cent of all executive jobs open were filled by means of announcements in the press. When we keep in mind that many of these posts are for junior 'executives' we have a glimpse of how small are the chances of success for anyone who has moved up significantly. Aside from the discouraging statistics, the competition clearly is the most fierce for posts that everyone knows about.

Many candidates are, of course, aware of the importance of the concealed 70 per cent of the market. However, this awareness is only the first step in a successful search. A prospector may know where a lode lies; extracting the gold is quite another matter.

I stress the two-step nature of the operation because many people attack the process in reverse. They blindly fire off, far and wide, canned CVs accompanied by a standard letter. They are, in effect, saying 'give me a job' rather than, simply, 'let's sit down and talk'. The exploratory part of their search has gone awry and they have burned the market through overexposure. By the time this hard-won knowledge sinks in, it is too late to recover the ground lost.

The thrust of what will follow should now be clear. The art of presenting oneself is first of all an art of making contacts. It is not a process of asking for a job. Once multiple meetings are arranged, the rest can follow.

However, be prepared. The quest for the best possible change of post inevitably demands an expenditure of time and energy. Please do not look here for samples of 'model' CVs or 'specimens' of letters. Just as you speak with your own unique voice and move about in your own way, so your way of putting yourself on paper must reflect your own personality, not that of some other person. If this authenticity is absent your correspondent will sense in a meeting that 'something feels wrong'; the person facing him or her is not the person he or she had been led to expect.

Instead of offering crutches, I will propose a kind of muscle-building exercise in the form of a very precise training in how to create the documents you will need. Many people later find that the principles that apply in a well-conducted search have useful applications in other kinds of public relations activity.

Meanwhile the subject of who you are is the right starting-point. So let us begin with a definition of the 'product' (you might as well face up to the word); namely, yourself.

Introduction

WHERE HAVE ALL THE 'JOBS' GONE?

The time has come to rethink every idea you have ever had about how to find the best jobs.

Restructuring. Downsizing. Outplacement. Re-engineering. These are among the scare words that monopolize the business climate of the 1990s. How come, then, that 94 per cent of the employables in Great Britain are listed as being gainfully employed?

A paradox? Perhaps. A mystery? Not at all, if we are ready to examine what is really happening in the so-called job market. To do so is not only important; it is essential to anyone, such as yourself, who wants to — or is forced to — find new employment.

Let us be blunt: the person who reactively waits for the 'right advertisement' to come along risks spending the remainder of his or her working life in front of the television. Even if one occasionally seems 'to have my name written on it', as some people put it, the same advert is a visible target for the hundreds of thousands of other 'job seekers' flooding the market today.

In 1988 only one third of jobs available were advertised. Today any such figure loses all meaning. The question no longer is whether 'jobs' are advertised but rather if they still exist in their traditional form. Yet somehow, out there in the dynamic, ever-changing world of modern enterprise, more gross national product (GNP) is being turned out than ever before. If not by people holding down regular jobs, by whom is it being performed?

Often the answer is, 'by outsiders'.

THE KNOWLEDGE WORKERS

Restructuring goes on as layers of middle-management fat are peeled away. We can even ask ourselves if a 'job market' in the old sense will even exist a few years from now. The nation's work is increasingly being performed by 'knowledge workers', outside experts hired under contract — sometimes as individuals, often as teams — to accomplish specific missions.

'Outsourcing' is the answer to 'where are the jobs going?' They are indeed going 'out'. The advantages to a company of outsourcing are enormous, of course. Flexibility in staffing is one. More important, functions calling for some particular expertise are likely to be better and more quickly performed by specialists in the matter. At the same time, the change also gives rise to new kinds of opportunities for career advancement, as we shall see.

How you can profit by swimming with this new tide, rather than against it, is partly what this book is about. But only partly. Many unpublicized 'permanent' salaried positions still become empty and need to be filled.

For two reasons these remaining, well-defined posts may be just as invisible to the public eye as those that have been outsourced. The reason is not hard to find. During periods of high unemployment, recruiters find themselves deluged with direct applications from highly motivated, competent people. Personnel people only have to reach into their files to find a reservoir of highly proactive candidates for almost any post. So why advertise?

In addition, the dwindling number of advertisements, chased by hoards of job hunters, is likely to generate an avalanche of correspondence. If only in the interest of good public relations, most respectable employers try to treat each application 'correctly', a labour-consuming and expensive business. (Some hire an executive search firm in order to remain anonymous. Or, in the case of routine positions, they might hire a 'recruiting agency', permitting them to hide behind an address that is little more than a postbox).

So dramatic are the changes under way that no one can hope to make sense of his or her working life without some understanding of what is happening. . .and, even more important, what is likely to happen. Your future wellbeing and that of your family may hang in the balance.

'TAKING THE VOWS'

We get a clearer view when we look back to the period between the two World Wars. In those days, most future management people married their company for life: 'for better or worse', and, one hoped, 'for richer' rather than poorer. In other words finding a 'permanent job' usually meant just that — an intended lifetime association. In the more patriarchal organizations, a certain mutual loyalty was taken for granted and served to bind employer and key employee together.

There were certain things that were 'just not done': for one, management did not boot key people out except as a last resort. If parting could not be avoided, a dischargee could expect a suitable period of notice together with a more-or-less generous sum of money to ease the pain of transition. Often the person was simply transferred from one department or division to another. For his part, a salaried employee was barred, if only by scruple, from selling his knowledge to the competition. In short, things tended to be done in a 'gentle-manly' way. (The use of the masculine in these two sentences is not accidental since women were then unlikely to be found in the ranks of management.)

Does all this sound rather quaint? That is hardly surprising; we are contemplating a world that exists no longer. That world started to evaporate shortly after the Second World War. Professional recruiters and human relations people began to look for some variety in the CVs of younger recruits. Three or four jobs to round out one's early experience were not only considered to be acceptable but came to be seen as a plus. By the 1960s 'the marriage for life' concept became as outmoded in the world of business as in the bedroom. Nevertheless, jobs were still encapsulated in clearly defined job descriptions and tucked into little squares in an organization chart.

THE SHAKE-OUT OF THE 1980s

The stage was set for the 1980s, ominously ushering in the most severe economic recession since the Second World War. No one who was in a company that reeled from the shock (and few did not) has to be reminded of the fall-out. Jolted, management woke up to the existence of layers of wasteful, overlapping functions that had accumulated during the fat years of prosperity. 'Downsizing' became a part of the business vocabulary. So did 'outplacement'. Jobs disappeared by the millions and among the prime targets for 'extrusion' were middle-managers who had built comfortable fiefs into the convolutions of ever more complex organization charts.

The effects of this wave of 'restructuring' are not at all invisible. William Bridges in his book *Job Shift* (Addison Wesley, New York, 1994) points out that nearly all of the jobs lost during previous recessions were reconstituted with the return to normal. But two years after the upturn from the recent recession in the US, only 18 per cent of the former job holders went back to their accustomed activities! Bridges goes on to cite estimates that 50 per cent of all jobs will never reappear at all in their past form.

In short, too many people seeking change today are charting their course while wearing blinkers because:

> On the one hand, they fail to recognize that many clearly-defined jobs like the ones they have held in the past no longer exist. The work they used to do is being performed in another fashion.
>
> On the other hand, they too-often rely on replying to adverts as a way to make a positive change.
>
> Yet the work is there to be done.

So much for the negative. Now on to the positive. While it is true that many jobs have been eliminated in both the private and public sectors, more work is being performed than ever before, as the GNP testifies. Partly the work is being turned out by smart machines; but nonetheless, 91.5 per cent of British employables are earning their keep while America has even fewer unemployed.

While this can seem mysterious, is it really? Bridges points out that we get closer to the truth when we replace the concept of 'having a job' with the idea of 'doing a job'. This is by no means simply quibbling about words; it is the key to many a successful career change.

Having a job describes the way most people have been earning their living for nearly 200 years — in other words, since the start of the Industrial Revolution. It was then that people left their farms and emerged from their crofts to become wage-earners in factories and offices. They went from performing a job of work, such as milking cows, to having a job; for example, as a coal miner.

WHAT IS A KNOWLEDGE WORKER?

People who do jobs rather than hold jobs are the knowledge workers. This means that they are putting to work what they know in a variety of ways. Inside an organization, they may often be found working in teams, perhaps to carry out a specific project, applying their knowledge and skills to what needs to be done on any particular project at any given time. There is no slot for them in an organization chart because there often is no organization chart. In a rapidly evolving industry, such as software, they move readily from project to project.

Otherwise, knowledge workers may work for subcontracting firms who are engaged by companies to perform the specific services they know best how to do. Major corporations are divesting themselves of whole departments, turning the work over to outside specialists. The list is impressive. For a long time it has included office maintenance, and more recently electronic data processing (EDP) installation and operations, executive relocation, employee training and direct marketing. (Let us not overlook executive recruiting, a speciality that has been around for 50 years.) It is hardly surprising that today the world's largest employer is Manpower Inc. More surprising is to read in the *International Herald Tribune* that more than 50 per cent of all employees can today be categorized as knowledge workers — either in-house or supplied from the outside. These are people who are mostly finding work outside the old framework of recognizable job descriptions.

A NUMBERS GAME

What does this revolution mean to anyone — such as yourself — who is at a career turning point? Precisely this:

■ Finding the right situation always has involved making contact with the greatest possible number of opportunities. More than ever today, it is a numbers game. However, now the targets are less easy to identify for the reasons we have spotlighted. How to reach this hidden market for your services is the subject of the chapters to come.

■ It is time to recognize that you are not — as perhaps in the past — 'asking for a job'. You are offering a service. What is sought in the new service-oriented economy is your knowledge and expertise rather than your agreeable personality and your ability to fit yourself into a rigid, rapidly outmoded corporate hierarchy. 'The Organization Man' is rapidly becoming a fossil.

■ Basically, selling your services rather than yourself is the difference between being a candidate for a 'job' and acting as your own entrepreneur. No longer is it a rule that a knowledge worker is restricted to serving one employer, though that, of course, may be the case. Maybe your best bet is to join a specialized firm contracting out its know-how to companies. Or you may choose to 'do it yourself' by renting out your knowledge directly to one or more company clients. A saying currently going the rounds states 'soon we all will be in business for ourselves'. This may be an exaggeration, but it conveys a basic truth.

■ The idea of developing an entrepreneurial outlook in regard to oneself may not gibe well with the nature of everyone seeking a change. For them, there is the 50 per cent of the market that consists of jobs in the traditional mould. But whichever direction is the right one for you, the same principle applies: you are selling a service in the form of your knowledge and skills.

To add this last particular skill to the others you already possess, read on. I assure you that you will find many uses later in your career for the techniques I have learned from working with hundreds of upwardly mobile managers. I am glad to have a chance to share them with you.

1

Who Are You?

So you want to change jobs.

But *why?*

Because you feel restless where you are and would like to 'look around'?

Because you have lost, or may be losing, your post and have to find another as soon as possible?

Or does your quest stem from a conviction that only a well-chosen change can offer you the career progression you seek?

No doubt what follows can be useful to people who find themselves in either of the first two categories — call them the restless and the breathless. But its greatest value will almost certainly be to the person who is now determined to take an important forward stride in his or her career.

You are 'just looking around'. For an executive who is 'just looking' the secrets contained in this book will at the very least help him or her to compare the reality of the present situation with the realities of the marketplace for his or her particular talents. It is evident that the position we hold today is real and tangible. We can measure the pros and weigh the cons in order to end up with a reasonably accurate balance sheet of the sources of our satisfaction and the reasons for our discontent. On the other hand, posts that exist perhaps 'out there' in the churning ever-volatile job market are hypothetical. They cannot be evaluated, obviously, until they have first been identified and then examined.

A well-organized job search can offer the restless executive what is perhaps his or her first opportunity to compare his or her present situation with others that actually exist. Only then, once in possession of firm job offers, can the questing executive judge accurately the wisdom of a move. Keeping in mind the inevitable risks of a change, he or she will want to compare salary with salary, title with title, potential for satisfaction with present satisfaction. Other variables include the possibility of progression and all of the factors that surround the word 'environment' (the quality of the product, geographical situation, the nature of one's future collaborators, etc). To move or not to move? Now the decision can be based on fact rather than on supposition.

You are under pressure to make a change. To the breathless job seeker, victim perhaps of a 'career accident' and desperately in need of a new situation, a well-organized and efficient exploration of the market may turn out to be something of a test of patience. However, I am convinced that a certain period of preparation is absolutely necessary before launching a vigorous attack. The expression 'more haste less speed' should become the motto of the person desperately seeking a solution to his or her problem. Not only will full attention to the suggestions that follow save time in the end but it will almost certainly produce more and better job offers. This consideration is especially important if one is to avoid the most dangerous trap awaiting the breathless chaser after 'a job'. I am speaking here of the temptation, so very understandable, to accept the first solid offer that comes along.

How good it is to be wanted after a period out in the cold — to be invited to join up with a team of productive human beings — rather than to go on trying to market oneself to seemingly smug types secure in their positions of control. You may well breathe a sigh of relief, saying 'finally the problem is solved'. But is it really, finally, solved?

Many managing directors are good salespeople — perhaps that is one of the reasons why they are in their job — and some executive search people also can wax overly enthusiastic about the client companies that retain (in other words, pay) them.

Thus a post may be painted in glowing colours as part of a process of seduction. Unhappily, six weeks later the gloss is sometimes gone, the situation proves a disappointment and the original problem not only still exists but it is compounded. You have cut your links with other potential employers. Returning to square one, now you must go back to a job market that you have already ransacked. How much better to have taken the time to generate several job offers through a co-ordinated attack — and so to have the opportunity to compare possibilities rather than to engage in a totalitarian election where you must say 'yes' or '*nyet*' to a single proposal.

In fact, one of the objects of this book is precisely that: to help rescue pressured people from their own natural impulses.

You are determined to seek the right next career move. Here we have the person who can profit most fully from a well-organized research of the possibilities that currently exist. Like the restless person, he or she wants to know what is 'out there'. However, such people bring to the quest important elements of motivation and determination that often are not found in the individual who is 'just looking around'.

My experience in career counselling confirms psychologist Daniel Levinson's studies of the mental and spiritual evolution of the adult male. Levinson identifies two important periods of change in the mature life not only of white-collar workers but also of labourers, artists and professional people. By 'periods of change' we mean certain phases of self re-examination, usually subconscious in their origin but very likely to be translated into some action intended to bring about an improvement in one's situation.

These 'passages' generally are first manifested between the ages of 28 to 32 and later between 38 and 42. The percentage of clients I receive who fall between these two age brackets is far beyond any statistical probability. These tend to be people who are prone to feel change as an inner imperative rather than (1) as an outgrowth of circumstance, such as the loss of a job, or (2) simply as the result of a vague feeling of boredom or restlessness, though these may be a part of the psychological mix.

The early-adulthood change. Members of the younger group, around the age of 30, are motivated by the need to coalesce and synthesize their experience to date with a view to optimizing in any way possible the future. More than two-thirds of their lifetime has been passed acting in accordance with, or reacting against, the influence of older, more experienced persons — chiefly parents and educators. Now comes a time of pragmatic testing, in the arena of real life, of one's education, training and experience. This person has passed through starting jobs and has now accumulated a significant number of skills. At the same time his or her personal life is maturing. He or she may well have established a household, probably with a mate, possibly with the addition of a child or two.

At this point certain questions make themselves felt rather than heard. 'On the one hand I have been taught how things are supposed to be, largely through the optic of other people. But also I now have the benefit of my own particular experience. The time has certainly come, before the course of my life becomes more fixed, to bring these two elements together, hopefully in the form of an activity which best promises to meet my own unique needs for satisfaction in my life in general and, in particular, in my work.'

In that paragraph lies the key to the most successful career changes. It clearly indicates the necessity for a double exploration: interior ('What are my real needs if I am to have job satisfaction?'); and exterior (the search of the job market for the right post).

The mid-life change. Similar factors are found in the early-adulthood change and the 'mid-life' transition. The questions a person puts to him or herself around the age of 40 are nonetheless quite different in nature from those faced by people of 30. The inner voice is likely to say, 'My life is about half over. Am I really as fulfilled as I could be? When I peer into the future what do I see — a slowing of growth, a gradual slide towards retirement or, on the contrary, the possibility of optimizing the second half in an activity that might offer me renewed opportunities for self-actualization?'

Thus once again the question of fulfilling our fundamental psychological and emotional needs in a work setting inevitably arises. Only through their satisfaction can we truly say we are happy in our work. The job search, then, becomes only part — the visible part — of an exploration that for many can be the most exciting adventure of their life. For those unprepared through a similar inner exploration the search risks becoming an exercise in frustration and rejection.

The essential first steps. From this introduction it is clear that there is preparatory work to be done before settling down to the challenging task of creating on paper your own image of yourself and, above all, of projecting that image in the most effective possible way to others. Failure to pass through the preliminary steps will almost certainly weaken your presentation of yourself. Your contacts by mail will suffer from the same thinness and lack of substance as would a printed advertisement prepared by a person who did not trouble to acquaint himself or herself with the product he or she is trying to sell.

No matter which of the above passages most closely corresponds to your own situation, I suggest you put to yourself a few key questions before you try to produce messages that you hope will open the right doors to an enriching future.

THE ASSETS INVENTORY

Not for the last time in this manual I must stress certain similarities between the challenge of introducing a new product into a highly competitive market and the act of making known, in the most positive way possible, your own availability. The conscious appreciation on your part of your own individual, characteristic merits is just as important — or perhaps even more important — to the result of your search as is the detailed product knowledge of the expert marketer to the outcome of his or her efforts.

With this principle in mind, I urgently suggest that you make it your first order of priorities — certainly before you attempt to produce written materials on the subject of yourself — to create an inventory of the qualities you see in yourself that represent potential assets to a future employer.

I am aware of the barriers that can present themselves as you undertake this task. 'What a waste of time! I certainly know my good points without bothering to write them down.' Or, 'What's the sense of writing out my strengths without noting also my weaknesses?' Or still again, 'How can one easily distinguish between a 'strength' and a 'weakness'? I'm an honest, open person. Is this good or bad? No doubt in some situations this works in my favour — in others, against me.' And so on.

Thus a negative process of intellectualization is set in motion (in which we may even take a certain pride). Carried to extremes, we conclude that a product or a service may well have qualities that are identifiable and 'marketable' but that I, a complex, marvellously wrought human being, can clearly identify none in myself.

In this manner the intellect can at times manifest itself as obstructionist — causing us to be 'sicklied o'r with the pale cast of thought'. On the other hand, used constructively, intelligent thought can represent our best key to self-knowledge. Thus I propose to you, not simply the creation of a list of what you perceive to be your strong points but also, after so doing, to view these same points through another prism. What indeed might be the opposite, negative, face of each merit? And, most enlightening, where does the balance lie between the two extremes? This is what figure-minded people inevitably call 'the bottom line'.

You will find here a radically new way of approaching a classic exercise: the evaluation of one's 'strengths' and 'weaknesses'. It is a method particularly adapted to what must be the first stage in any effective job search — the presentation of yourself on paper. This becomes an exercise in self-identity. However, in terms widely used today, it is vital to see 'the glass as half full rather than half empty'. In other words, let us give first priority to the qualities we actually possess — the strong points that constitute our positive contributions to a future employer.

Only after arriving at a clear recognition of these assets is it useful to consider any shortcomings that might represent targets for self-improvement. Let me be especially clear on this point: what is not 'realism' is to start out by focusing on weak points that need to be corrected. Well-meaning parents and teachers often have taken this approach throughout our formative years. While the motive of such negative instruction has been 'improvement', the effect can be singularly unhelpful at precisely the time when you are obliged to put your best foot forward.

It will be apparent that the assets we are to deal with here are exclusively aspects of one's personality and character. Your specialized knowledge — perhaps technical or scientific — can become in some situations equally important as part of the total 'package' you have to offer. Both age and level of management are key factors in weighing the relative importance of your human values versus your specialized knowledge.

We can generalize by saying that nearly everyone at the start of his or her working life is hired to perform some specialized task; possessing, in effect, readily identifiable knowledge to sell — for example in the fields of accounting, sales or engineering. However, with each upward step in the corporate hierarchy the pendulum of his or her value to the organization swings away from such circumscribed contributions and towards his or her abilities in human relations.

One interesting, and often valuable, way to view the relative importance of technical skills versus human qualities is as follows:

The effective utilization of specialized knowledge early in the career can be enhanced or diminished by the relative presence or absence of skills in human relations. . .

but. . .

specialized knowledge becomes less important than skills in human relations with each upward step in the evolution of one's career.

In assessing your own mix of innate and specialized qualities you have no choice but to seek them within yourself using all the objectivity you can muster. If you are project manager for a construction company, your engineering know-how obviously will be vastly more important to your marketability than such technical knowledge would be to a sales manager of hand tools.

However, let me stress once again, your strengths as a human being are a constant, positive factor. They are your basic stock in trade and largely will determine your performance in any kind of post you hold or for which you may be looking.

So saying, I now suggest that you proceed to a reflection on your best qualities. To help launch this exercise — to 'prime the pump' of your thinking — you will find below a list of 15 possible qualities that I have ascribed to some imaginary person. Among them may be assets you recognize in yourself. Include in your own list those that apply to yourself, but in addition add as many others as you may think of. To do this work, I suggest you distance yourself from the telephone, the television and the children in order seriously to address yourself to a frequently difficult question: 'What's good about me?'.

- Good health/high energy.
- Loyal.
- Tenacious.
- Diplomatic.
- Analytical.
- Optimistic/positive.
- Good people contact.
- Good written communications.
- Rigorous.
- Intuitive intelligence/rapid decision maker.
- Creative.
- Adaptable.
- 'Self-starter'.
- Well read/wide culture.
- Good appearance.

THE LAW OF OPPOSITES

To arrive at such a list of the good qualities one possesses can be soothing to the ego; it also can be dangerously misleading because of the absolute, categorical nature of such words. It takes but little reflection to see that even a quality as admirable as rigour can have its inconvenient aspects, particularly in situations where a certain flexibility is important. In its positive manifestations rigour can inspire the confidence and admiration of others. When we apply the Law of Opposites, however, this praiseworthy characteristic is seen to be a potential handicap.

Likewise, we all know people who display a kind of directness and 'honesty' in their relations with others, seldom hesitating to point out their errors or weaknesses. Masquerading as an effort to be 'helpful', such behaviour can simply prove to be abrasive.

Yet it would be an error to regard the Law of Opposites as solely an exercise in extremes, with absolute merit resting at one extreme and thoroughly negative comportment at the other. As is the case with everything pertaining to human nature, nuances exist — subtle shadings between snow-white and funereal black.

You will find illustrations of such gradations in Figure 1.1. At the left I have listed the qualities that I cited on page 30 as examples of some typical assets. Then moving to the right along each line, I have traced degree by degree their diminution in terms of their fullest exploitation. Finally, to the right of the vertical centre line, the point is reached where these very same characteristics cease to be assets and risk to become troublesome.

'A great quality, but. . .'. You can continue for yourself this exercise in the evaluation of your own particular qualities. So you are a person who can make quick, intuitive decisions. Fine, but ask yourself, 'Am I sometimes impulsive, not taking time to think through tough problems before acting?' You are a good delegator. Splendid, but do you sometimes place too much confidence in your subordinates — to your later regret? And so on.

Tenacious	Persists in problem-solving	Sticks long with hopeless projects	Stubborn
Diplomatic	Good at resolving conflicts	'Harmony' high in priorities	Overly agreeable
Optimistic	But also realistic	Forecasts sometimes too high	Can misjudge risk
Energetic	Always keeps fit	Nearly always keeps fit	Keeps too long hours
Loyal	Some years with each company	Unreasonably long with same company	Loves the boss
Analytical	Decisions based on fact	Spurns role of intuition	Coldly cerebral
Good contact	Persuasive, has charm	Well-liked on all levels	Gregarious
Writes well	Persuasive on paper	Prefers communication in writing	Too lavish with memos
Rigorous	Strong, determined	Controls large and small matters	Overly controlling
Intuitive	Can make quick decisions	Prefers intuition to reflection	Often too spontaneous
Creative	By nature an innovator	Often produces realistic ideas	Has trouble selling ideas
Adaptable	Readily fits in	Absorbs first, then adapts	Adapts but slowly
'Self-starter'	Needs no bossing, gets on with job	Shows initiative when needed	Hesitates but then acts
Well informed	Has large bank of useful information	Keeps abreast of events	Cultured
Good appearance	Attractive, impressive	Dresses correctly, carries self well	A bit too fastidious

Figure 1.1 *The Law of Opposites*

Note: Two notable omissions from the above chart are 'honest' and 'hard worker'. Happily these qualities are so common as to be deprived of a claim to distinction. They are assumed to exist.

Defends lost causes	Does not know when to quit	Impedes progress	**Obstructionist**
Avoids conflict	Dithers	Lacks courage	**Gives up quickly**
Overly trusting	Takes too many chances	Loses trust of superiors	**Disillusioned**
Often overworks	Constantly overworks	Stressed out	**Overwhelmed by work**
Dependent on boss	'Used' by boss	Drudges along	**Self-sacrificing**
Few concrete results	Bores colleagues	Impedes action	**Loses human contact**
Relies on charm	Likes to gossip	Resists tough jobs	**Seen as lightweight**
Lacks spontaneity	Long hours 'pen in hand'	Distant with colleagues	**Works best in isolation**
Overbearing	'Perfectionist'	Irritates people	**Relationship problems**
Decides then justifies	Short-term thinker	Not good with figures	**Defends actions badly**
Poor at selling ideas	Ideas lack practicality	Flits from one idea to another	**Always seems distracted**
Agrees too readily	Restless when no change	Changes jobs frequently	**Changes jobs too often**
Overly autonomous	Fails to report upwards	Resents authority	**Problems with management**
Overly cerebral	Lacks pragmatism	Intellectually snobbish	**Has trouble integrating**
May seem superficial	Expects admiration of others	Uses 'seduction' to advance	**Relies mostly on good looks**

What is clear is that your strengths, not their opposites, are the characteristics that should dominate both your conscious mind as well as (to the extent possible) your subconscious mind as you launch on your job search. Not only will your intelligent, objective appreciation of your strong points convey itself through your way of presenting yourself on paper and in person, but your knowledge of the precise degree to which these valuable qualities dominate their own caricatures will prove a real aid to your self-confidence.

HOW TO APPLY THE LAW OF OPPOSITES TO YOURSELF

The random list of characteristics shown in Figure 1.1 is intended only to stimulate your own thinking. You are at liberty, of course, to borrow from it any qualities you find in yourself. However, the list you finally arrive at should reflect as closely as possible your own unique panoply of attributes.

At the left side of the page characterize each quality in its most desirable manifestation. (For example, the person who is 'diplomatic' might be 'good at resolving conflicts'. Then at the far right indicate the most negative evidence of the same characteristic (perhaps, 'avoids conflict at all cost').

Once you have listed the extremes on opposite sides of the paper, you can proceed — moving from left to right — to fill in the six descending gradations, as I have done. Your chart should, finally, comprise a total of at least 15 characteristics listed vertically and analysed horizontally for their degree of, or lack of, desirability.

Now I suggest you arm yourself with a pen or pencil that writes in green and another in red. Frame with green ink each categorization of yourself that you find situated to the left of the vertical centre line. To the right of the line outline in red the rectangles, if any, that you feel are descriptive of yourself.

The result? The boxes in green now give you a precise inventory of the human qualities that promise to aid your career advancement. These are what you have to 'sell'. Evidently each quality is rated — not in absolute terms — but in accordance with its relative importance. At the same time the characteristics framed in red — those to the right of the centre line — may prove just as vital in terms of self-knowledge. They constitute clear directional signals pointing out your specific targets for improvement.

Is change possible? In passing, I agree with those who maintain that the basic human stuff within us remains constant throughout our lifetime. This represents our precious individuality which some people feel is bestowed from on high or at least from our genes. Such a statement, however, by no means eliminates the possibility of positive modification in our ways of behaving.

Certainly the indispensable start of such a process is to recognize our unproductive habits. Thereafter, constant awareness of their tendency to recur, plus a zeal to move them to the left of your chart, can produce transformations for the better.

Up to this point I have been proposing that you put certain questions to yourself in order to raise the level of your self-knowledge when facing an important career change. The next question speaks for itself: 'How do we put that self-knowledge to work in a successful job search?'

For the answers, read on. . .

2

Setting the Stage

Why do so many job searches, often conducted by people with impressive qualifications, fall short of the results hoped for? A major reason, in my opinion, is the common tendency to think in terms of too small numbers.

We can test out this statement by looking at the likely results of a typical mailing designed to contact companies and executive search firms. Let us visualize a middle-management executive with a good performance record and an acceptable diploma, who is between 28 and 48. (The minimum figure of 28 is based on the fact that relatively few people can fully justify the title 'executive' earlier than that. The upper figure represents an age when rising salary expectations typically tend to level off.)

We will further assume for the moment that the letters which go out are properly targeted and well done.

When these conditions are met, a candidate can typically expect a total response from companies and executive search firms of around 50 per cent. 'Total' includes negative, positive and noncommittal replies. The number of positive responses in the mix is likely, on average, to amount to 10 per cent. I define as 'positive' any response that proposes some concrete action on your part: 'Fill out the enclosed form', 'Send along a CV', 'Phone for an appointment'.

Normally about half of the positive replies will result in interviews. Now it becomes apparent that a good mailing of

100 letters may produce five meetings. Therein lies the problem. Five interviews is just not enough to assure a successful result.

Am I being unnecessarily downbeat? Not in the light of my figures which show that six out of seven first interviews will fail to produce a satisfactory job offer. Either you may not like what you learn about the job or the interviewer finds that you are not the person for whom he or she is looking. Thus, statistically, you can count on having not much more than one concrete offer.

INCREASING YOUR CHANCES

An offer — but is it the best one?

So what's wrong with that? 'After all, I'm only looking for one post!' To my mind everything is wrong. You say yes or you say no to that particular offer, but you have had no chance to compare one tangible possibility against another — or others. As a result you cannot be sure you are accepting the post that is the best one available to you.

'By the same token', the protest continues, 'you can never be sure to have those "one or more" offers in hand at more or less the same time. If you must reach a decision on one in October and another offer comes along in December, you might as well forget about comparisons. You have to decide to accept or not the first opportunity — or let the first one slip away because of your procrastination.'

We are now moving into the subject of methods available in the conduct of a well-managed job search. There exist ways of dealing with such a time lag just as there are techniques for creating effective job-search materials. Later on we will deal with the nuts and bolts of a productive campaign. For the moment, my point is simple and clear: by increasing the number of contacts by mail you will multiply the number of person-to-person contacts. In turn you will, correspondingly, reap more concrete job offers.

Suppose you triple your mailings. Instead of 100, you choose 300 well-selected targets. Applying the 10 per cent rule, you can expect 30 positive replies, half of which will turn into interviews. On average, three offers will result. In itself, this may not appear to be a brilliant result. However, contacting people by mail is by no means the only method of exploration available. Later we will spell out other, reinforcing actions to enrich the results, including networking, personal contacts and, on rare occasions, responses to advertising. All important is *how* each of these steps is conceived and put into action — a part of the discussion to come.

The CV — a dangerous instrument

But first let us avoid any risk of misunderstanding at the outset. When I refer to 'approaches by mail' I am in no way focusing on the common practice of sending out CVs far and wide. Even the best CV is a dangerous instrument. In the words of one career consultant, 'no one ever hired a CV'. I am alarmed at the fixation most candidates have on producing the perfect document. In fact, often they seem to be intent on selling the CV rather than themselves. Obviously a candidate must be armed with a good CV — to be presented at the proper time. The CV presented prematurely risks being used, particularly by personnel people, more as an instrument to 'screen out' candidates rather than to screen them in. Each detail risks pointing to some element that does not jibe with the idealized job description the recruiter has in mind and so leads to the 'no' file.

THE QUESTION OF CONFIDENTIALITY

Any discussion of a widespread job search often sets off alarm signals in the mind of the candidate who is still employed.

'Suppose', he or she might say, 'word gets back to my management that I am "out on the market".' In the case of a few companies — including one of the giants in household products — such a fear might be justified. The American company I have in mind regards such 'disloyalty' in itself sufficient ground for firing.

In most cases, however, the fear is exaggerated; most of us tend to overestimate our importance to our organization. Likewise it is natural to imagine ourselves as the focus of more attention than is really the case.

The candidate in hiding

Where such fear really is justified, the possibility of masking your identity does exist. This can be accomplished either by using a post office box number or by arranging with a career consulting firm to write about you on their stationery without mention of your name. Such dodges have only one drawback: they are not nearly as successful as the direct approach. Evidently most companies are hesitant to deal with someone who seems to be hiding.

When you are in danger of becoming blocked on the question of anonymity, you should consider two cases where news of a job search somehow leaked back to an individual's management. Far from being a disaster, the result in each instance turned out to be highly favourable to the individual and to his company.

The first of these concerned an American — let us call him Alec — working in Scotland in the subsidiary of a US company. By nature a take-charge person, Alec found himself sidetracked into a non-operational post as marketing co-ordinator. Stifled, he felt he had to change and mailed a number of exploratory letters to US companies. One of them fell into the hands of his own corporate CEO in New York. As it happened, this man had been Alec's boss ten years earlier in the company's Canadian subsidiary.

The big boss was furious, but not with Alec. He faulted the manager in Scotland for his failure to make full use of the abilities that the CEO knew Alec possessed. Summoned to New York, Alex was assigned to study potential of a new product line in the Middle East market. He was subsequently installed in Athens as area manager for the eastern Mediterranean region. This was exactly the kind of situation he had been seeking on the outside.

Paul's round trip

Then there is the case of an insurance executive I will call Paul. Paul had been stationed for five years in Japan. During his time there he married a Japanese and became an avid student of Zen. Back in the home office in London, he and his wife found themselves (as have many other returnees) disoriented and nostalgic for the Far East. He began a search of possibilities and was rewarded with an offer from a maritime assurance company to head up their Hong Kong branch. However, a surprise awaited Paul when he broke the news of his acceptance to his own company.

'Why didn't you share your feelings openly with us?' his managing director asked. 'The board has been discussing a move into Taiwan. You would have been an excellent candidate to pioneer this venture.'

In the end, an embarrassed Paul went back to the maritime people and pulled out of his agreement with them. Six months later he and his wife were in the air headed for Taiwan.

'What's this I hear?'

These histories are not intended to deny that confidentiality is essential in some situations. However, the possibility of leakage always will exist. But even if such an awkward moment does actually arrive, this is not necessarily a disaster. Certainly a lot depends on how each individual handles the situation. Your first order of business is to learn precisely what information the questioner possesses.

'What's this I hear?' this person might say. 'I understand you are looking around for another job.'

Instead of taking the defensive, you might respond with a question: 'What makes you think that?'

If his or her reply is along the lines: 'There are rumours to that effect', you could answer truthfully: 'That's probably because, like a lot of people, I have recently been in touch with a couple of headhunters.'

This truthful reply leaves open the question of who took the initiative: the executive search firms or yourself.

A more difficult scenario is one in which your boss may wave a letter you have written to some company. In such a case, you would be well-advised to say (again truthfully): 'I have been told that it makes sense for a person to explore the job market at intervals in his career in order to compare his current level of progress with what's potentially out there. Do you yourself feel this kind of a practical career check-up makes sense?'

The important element in my suggested replies is to avoid any statement that might be construed as a resignation. Further on we will discuss the tactics of departure, focusing on the relative merits of being 'fired' or resigning.

Meanwhile, the thrust of this discussion of 'confidentiality' is clear: in deciding whether to expand or restrict the number of your contacts, lean in the direction of expansion rather than contraction. To a large extent an effective job search becomes a numbers game.

CONTROLLING THE TIME FACTOR

Earlier I identified another common objection to thinking generously in terms of numbers of contacts; namely, that the concept is flawed. 'What's the point of going after multiple job offers', they say, 'when they are almost bound to be strung out over a period of time? You'll have to say "yes" or "no" to the first one that ripens.'

In practice, that is not the way a well-conducted mail campaign works. One key — but not the only one — to controlling the cadence of your exploration is to recognize that certain types of approaches are slower-acting than others.

In terms of speed of reaction to your approach — starting with the swiftest — the following sequence is typical:

1. Letters written directly to top people in companies.
2. Letters to intermediaries such as executive search and recruiting firms.
3. Letters to key people based on items about them that have appeared in the press.*
4. Letters requesting a meeting to solicit advice (rather than to propose a candidacy).
5. Overtures to friends and other personal contacts.

In terms of timing, your mailings should take into account these varying speeds of reaction. Reversing this list in order to start your campaign with the slowest reacting technique, we come up with the following cadence of mailings:

1. Overtures to friends and contacts (see Chapter 9).
   — One week later, mailing to obtain:
2. Advice visits (see Chapter 9).
   — Two weeks later, mailing to obtain:
3. Meetings with executive search firms (see Chapter 4).
   — Two weeks later, mailing to obtain:
4. Meetings with companies (see Chapter 6).

Everyone agrees that people are not products and some job seekers even resent the idea that certain principles apply to both. However, we have already set out some guidelines that sound very much like elements of a marketing plan, and the success-oriented executive will continue to maintain his or her objectivity. In fact, certain fundamental mistakes are to be

---

* Any letter inspired by 'help wanted' advertising or the names of interesting targets appearing in news items will, of course, be sent out as the occasion arises.

avoided at the outset of a job-seeking campaign as assiduously as a marketing director will avoid promoting air-conditioners in Helsinki in December. So let us now sum up these taboos before moving on to the creation of the sales tools you are going to need in order to promote that most unique of all 'products' — yourself.

3

Taxiing to Take-off

You are the advertising director of a company producing quality consumer goods. You have an advertising budget of £10 million — half of which is to be spent in the print media. Your printed advertising must attract readers first of all; and in the end, it must also produce sales. Otherwise you will find yourself seeking another way to earn your keep.

One night after a good dinner, cognac in hand, you dash off a few lines and stuff them into envelopes to go to the advertising departments of a half-dozen leading magazines with instructions to publish.

Or let us try another equally unlikely scenario. You sit back and await inspiration. It fails to arrive with the second, or even the third, brandy. After midnight you give up and turn in, hoping for better luck tomorrow.

When the challenge is one of self-marketing, these extremes — impulsiveness on the one hand, impotence on the other — are all too common. They are in sharp contrast with the objectivity that marks a professional advertising campaign. There the writer can weigh the product, measure it and judge its merits with a high degree of accuracy.

Even so, only someone who has felt the anguish of creativity among the professionals can understand the thought — the careful weighing of each nuance — that lies behind the seemingly casual phrases that finally find their way into print.

The reason for such an investment of time and effort is clear to all involved in the process. It comes down to a matter of the figures at stake — let us say an expenditure of £5 million. Why, then, should not a similar pragmatism mark an executive job search? After all, the earnings over the next ten years of a person earning £40,000 a year come to an impressive figure, particularly when perks are thrown in. For most people, £500,000 more or less represents a sum to be treated with respect.

THE OBJECTIVE ELEMENTS

Granted that achieving objectivity in regard to ourselves is not easy, still, the effort must be made. Only after both the product and its potential market have been defined clearly can the process of putting words to paper be undertaken with any degree of confidence. Chapter 1 began such an exploration but there are ponderable factors to be inventoried in addition to our strengths of personality and character. Among them are certain ponderable matters that should also be held clearly in mind.

Here is a suggested checklist:

- Level of education.
- Quantifiable accomplishments registered during career.
- Career progress, step by step.
- Interesting activities outside career.

An equally vital next step involves looking outward rather than inward. Where in the wide world of work is there a need of the kind of product you will be offering? Or, in more specific terms, what kinds of position promise to offer you maximum job satisfaction and progress? (If you feel that making money is your only goal, what follows may not be of much interest to you. But, beware; work that produces no inner rewards is not likely, in the long run, to be well rewarded in terms of income.)

The moment of job change is the time to ask yourself two kinds of question. First, in what sphere of activity would you choose (if you could) to pass your working hours? The second question is, how practical is it for you to hope to find a decently paid post in such a setting?

Chapter 2 examines the question of how to time the various steps in a typical job search. 'Typical', however, is a word that seldom applies to ourselves. A good example is the degree of change a person is seeking — or thinks would be possible. To a greater or lesser extent we are all prisoners of our past. A person who started out as a chartered accountant and then moved upwards in financial management is hardly likely to win out in the competition for a post of sales director.

Nearly everyone has some idea of the kinds of product or service for which he or she can feel some degree of enthusiasm. This is innate and closely linked to your own nature. You may already be working in an activity you find satisfying. Inevitably your search is likely to focus on enterprises doing work similar to that which you have already found you like. Even so, this is the time to weigh all possible alternatives.

SOLO BRAINSTORMING

Brainstorming is usually done in groups. However, there is a way that an individual with a mind receptive to all of the grand possibilities that exist in the world of work can engage in: a kind of do-it-yourself brainstorming. First comes input of information. For starters, here is a sampling of some products and services towards which people might gravitate. Ask yourself which of them, if any, 'speaks to you' positively:

■ Large industrial products like cranes and earth-movers.
■ Small, intricate objects such as watches.
■ Fashions, including fabrics.
■ Food products and preparation.
■ Hi-tech products.

- Things that move: automobiles, airplanes, locomotives.
- Buildings: homes and offices.
- Hotels.
- Management consulting.
- Printed products: books, magazines.
- Television.

Since the world is 'so full of a number of things', this list is only a start in consulting yourself as to your own preferences. For a complete checklist of the various kinds of enterprises doing business today, obtain a copy of the *Standard Industrial Classification (SIC)* list from your bookseller, library or chamber of commerce. With this list, you will be able to make certain that all interesting targets for your search-to-come will be taken into account.

Lucille's story

On the other hand, we can visualize situations where there exists a deep-seated motivation to change. One of the most difficult challenges faces many women who seek to break through the 'glass ceiling' of promotion — usually out from the secretarial ranks. Simply because of the difficulty of bringing off this kind of change let us look at the situation of Lucille Larkin.

Armed with a liberal arts degree from London, Lucille Larkin quickly learned that the only kind of work she stood a chance of finding was as a secretary. So she took a course to learn typing and word processing. Over the next ten years, Lucille made progress but always as a sort of 'girl Friday' in a brokerage firm in the city. To stave off boredom, she worked hard to perfect what she loved best — her oil painting. She not only signed up for a course in drawing and painting; but she also studied French because of her firm's involvement with the Continent. In her job, she went through the classic evolution — from stenographer to secretary to 'assistant'. All along she knew the best of her talents was going unused. This was her good way with people, linked with a high level of persuasion.

Then came downsizing and she found herself working for three bosses instead of one. The pressures of time and the simultaneous demands from the members of her trio for work to be turned out 'right away' were too much. She resolved to make a change. By that time she realized that her repeated courses in mastering new computer techniques were an asset. But what kind of change could liberate her from slavery to bosses and electronic machines?

The situation clearly called for marshalling the classic steps of brainstorming to bring to light an array of future possibilities — perhaps more or less realistic, perhaps more or less desirable. The problem: she had no group with which to interact. Then she learned that there was a way to 'storm' her own brain. First — and absolutely essential — first step is to inventory one's assets. What does she *know* and what can she *do*. The next requirement is an open mind; that is, resisting the human temptation to say 'no' to any thought that might bubble up. The second step is to reverse this indiscriminate, affirmative process to reject those choices that are clearly unrealistic. At this stage, perhaps 10 or 12 alternatives are left that merit serious consideration. You will find Lucille's choices listed in Figure 3.1.

The final step is to rank the validity of each in comparison with the others. This can be done visually, as shown in Figure 3.1. Very important is to realize that the scores shown on the chart represent the *relative* rating of each possibility versus the others. (For example, No 6, art editor, is rated 40 per cent for 'realism'. This does not mean that Lucille had a 40 per cent chance of landing such a job. Rather that No 6 appears less realistic than No 9, administering a language school.)

Wishes versus practicality, seeking the balance

The chart shown in Figure 3.1 is easy to create but requires reflection to execute properly.

Step 1. As shown, rule off the chart in ten percentiles from 10 at the bottom to 100 at the top. At each of these intervals draw a horizontal line across the chart. Follow the same procedure moving from left to right, ruling off vertical lines, again in ten percentiles, from 10 to 100.

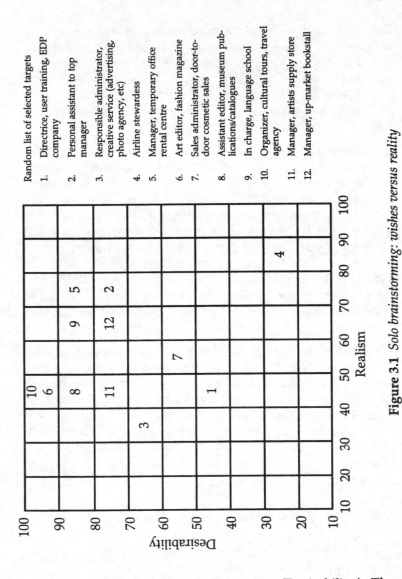

Figure 3.1 *Solo brainstorming: wishes versus reality*

Step 2. Mark the vertical dimension 'Desirability'. Then label the horizontal segment 'Realism'.

Step 3. On a separate sheet, list all of the uncensored ideas that occur to you. Discard those that are obviously impractical. Then on the right side list the remaining positions — without regard for their realism. Number each one. Typically a list would now total 10 or 12 possibilities.

Step 4. Now you are ready to undertake an evaluation of each of the possibilities you have listed. Starting with number 1 on your list, reflect first on what attracted you to such an activity (its 'desirability') and then on your opinion of the reality of such a move. If a possibility appears, for example, to be 50 per cent desirable and 50 per cent realistic in the light of the job market, place the number 1 in the box that represents the intersection of 50 per cent vertically and 50 per cent horizontally. Continue the process number by number as listed, through to the end of your list.

Step 5. You now have before you a scatter chart of numbers. It quickly becomes evident that the numbers that fall in the upper right quadrant are the best combination of realism and desirability. For the top five or six possibilities, add the percentage scores, horizontal and vertical, for each. The result will produce clearly three targets you are well advised to select for exploration.

Lucille's choice

True to the kind of widespread job search soon to be described here, Lucille spread her net widely, but focused on the four best combinations that fell in the upper right quadrant of the chart: in charge, language school; manager, temporary office rental centre; manager, up-market bookstall; and personal assistant to top manager. Her problem was finally solved by accepting the number 2 spot in a fast-growing temporary office rental centre to understudy the manager who wanted to be liberated to move on to a larger complex that was a part of the same chain of such centres. She was able to use fully her excellent contact with clients and prospects, her wide knowledge of electronic office machines (enabling her to train new staff), and the administrative skills she had acquired up to then. Her French and her refined taste in office decor were added pluses.

FIRST, SOME DO NOTS

Before examining various kinds of written materials that will launch your exploration, let us clear the decks with some 'do nots' in order to eliminate certain gremlins at the start.

Do not use window envelopes. A well-conducted research of the job market involves a lot of contacts by mail. Some of my more ingenious clients have hit on the window envelope as a time-saver since it eliminates the need to address envelopes. This may be rational thinking, but beware! The fact is that this device can boomerang, as I can verify from my experience with clients who have fallen into this trap. Just why window envelopes are ill-received I am not quite sure. Do people assume they usually contain advertising or, even less welcome, bills? For whatever reason, they seem to engender a subconscious resistance. As a result, the rate of response from a mailing can be halved in comparison with the 50 per cent response rate normally expected from a traditional mailing.

Beware of 'originality'. Large black type, garish colours, tapes, messages on cardboard or on over-sized sheets of paper — all these and other 'original' ways have been used to try to attract attention. Perhaps they succeed, but the attention they attract is largely negative. Such tricks almost never produce a positive reply.

Avoid metered mailings. Beware of the convenience of using a postage meter — whether at home or through the post office. It is the quickest way to signal to the addressee that you are mailing in quantity. This can be particularly troublesome if you have risked marking the envelope 'confidential or 'personal'. Metered postage simply serves to make a joke of your claim to special attention. The cardinal rule, in this matter and in all other respects, is that your message must appear to be directed to a single person, the recipient, even though he or she is perfectly aware that this is not the case.

Do not sign with black ink. Use dark blue instead in order to avoid the appearance of a printed signature — again in the interest of individualizing each letter.

Do not send handwritten letters. Even on the threshhold of the twenty-first century, some people still cling to the eighteenth century way of communicating. They explain that it is 'warmer', 'more personal' and 'less mechanical' to write than to use a typewriter or wordprocesser. Whatever the grain of truth in such arguments, they are overshadowed by one major consideration: both executive recruiters and busy managers generally receive an enormous amount of mail — including communications from job seekers. Anyone who has ever found him or herself trying to decipher a batch of handwritten letters knows the waste of time involved. Inevitably the resulting irritation generates a less than receptive mood.

Having now disposed of the 'do nots', let us move on quickly to the 'dos', focusing first on the art of creating a motivating letter likely to produce, as its name implies, action.

4

The Motivating Letter

Do you want to change your kind of work? Or perhaps you are devoted to the career path you have been on and you seek to continue in it.

Your answer is important. If you wish to proceed along a straight line from past to future, your CV (see Chapter 5 for more on this subject) becomes a central marketing tool. The path is clearly marked. An assistant chief accountant becomes chief, and finally is made financial director. A regional sales manager moves up to sales manager and then perhaps to marketing director. And so on: each new post contains ingredients of the last — only, one hopes, in a richer mixture. In achieving this kind of progression, executive recruiters may often turn out to be your allies. If they can see you doing in the future what you have done in the past — only more so — they can readily sell your past experience to their client.

FORCED OR UNFORCED?

To change your sector of activity or your function is quite another matter. Obviously this is the greater challenge. At the same time, widening your target is bound to open up a greater range of possibilities. Sometimes the reason for seeking a change of career is because one is 'fed up' with a lack of job satisfaction. Or, increasingly, there may be little choice; today's rapidly changing management practices mean that many people find themselves forced to change. Some people are not simply out of a job; in fact, the 'job' itself no longer exists. It was among the many management posts that downsizing has wiped from the organization chart. Examples abound. Quality control is no longer likely to be the concern of a single individual; rather, it has become everyone's responsibility. The after-sales manager may well find that his customer relations have been 'jobbed out' (or 'outsourced') to a service that formerly did nothing but deliver the merchandise. Management information services may now be in the hands of an outside group of specialists; and so on.

TWO DIFFERENT MEASURES

Like executive search people, personnel managers also tend to categorize candidates by set job descriptions. They prefer CVs that 'match up' with what they perceive to be their company's existing needs. They are likely to give the nod to someone who has a good record in such and such clearly defined function and possessing compatible product experience.

Managing directors, on the other hand, can — even must — be more creative. They know that risk can pay off. They also have in mind the whole panorama of the present and future functioning of their organization. They want to know what knowledge the individual possesses *today* and what he or she is *capable of doing*. Whereas the professional recruiter tends to base judgements on a candidate's 'experience' (though perhaps somewhat outdated) top managers know that current knowledge is what counts.

There can be no fixed 'rules' for bringing about career change by means of a motivating letter.[*] Nevertheless, certain basic principles are important.

---

[*] For information about to whom to address your motivating letter, see the listing of references in the Appendix.

Principle no 1: is not to ask for a job. Your objective is to arrange a meeting based on some mutual interest between yourself and the person you are addressing.

Principle no 2: this is not a letter to outline your career history — in other words, a sort of CV in letter form. It speaks of what you *can do* rather than detailing at length what you have done in the past. (Everybody has 'experience'; not everyone has competence!)

Principle no 3: keep it short, occupying a maximum of one page with generous margins.

THE CASE OF ROLAND ROE

That sets the stage. Refinements will be discussed later. But for the moment you can best see how the motivating letter functions by glancing at an actual case history — that of Roland Roe. (Not his real name, of course. Other details also have been modified to protect anonymity.)

Roland Roe was disillusioned with the diplomatic career his father had urged on him. Though in the fast lane in the foreign service, he was now assigned to the African desk in London. He found he missed the travel and variety he had had before his reassignment. In fact, the constant changes had helped him to stifle his growing conviction that the life of a public servant was not for him. He found it lacked creativity and tangible results. For a person of Ronald's nature, career success was linked too closely to servility. Clearly his father had, with the best of good will, set him off on the wrong track. Now, at the age of 35, Roland resolved to try to enter the world of business.

He sought the advice of certain classmates from Cambridge who were in business or finance. Their reaction was unanimous. With varying degrees of gentleness they inferred that he was barmy even to consider a change. Not only did he have no experience in the rough and tumble of business but his current situation would be the envy of most people. 'Stay put and be thankful', they advised.

Roland was not ready to give up so easily. He had heard of some out-fits that people referred to as headhunters. Certain that they would have a more professional, objective view, he created a CV — rather a good one, he thought — and sent it out to a dozen executive search firms. In his résumé he pointed out his experience in the four developing countries to which he had been posted. He stressed that he had become embassy secretary at an unusually young age. And, of course, he mentioned his second from Cambridge.

Polite letters were the response but nothing more. Undaunted, he telephoned several of the people he had written to and succeeded in arranging three appointments. However, even among these professionals, the advice was the same: 'forget the possibility of a change'. His profile, they told him was indelibly that of a promising junior diplomat. And, furthermore, did he realize fully how lucky he was to have a good job carrying such prestige and security? However, the last person he spoke with did mention the name of a consultant in personal career development. He shrugged, 'Still, I doubt even they can do anything in a case like yours.'

That was how I came to know Roland. By the time we met his confidence was a bit shaken. 'They may be right,' he said. 'I may well have to face up to it; I have no particular skills to offer. After all, I'm only a generalist.'

This was not the first (or the last time) I have heard people bemoan that they are 'only a generalist'. I suggested to Roland that in some situations this might be seen as a strength rather than a weakness. (After all, even the label 'general management' hints at the value of a broad background.) Using that as a starting-point, we emerged with a letter stressing the positive side of Roland's background to be addressed directly to the managing directors of companies with holdings abroad. I insisted that no CV be sent. The letter was more or less as follows:

Dear Mr _____

The nature of your company's international activities, as well as my own background and interests, suggests that there is common ground between us.

We face a two-way challenge well known to both of us: this is to maintain solid contact between a home office and its local representatives; and to assure continuing good relations on the ground with both the governmental and local authorities.

Since leaving Cambridge I have been actively involved in such concerns.

Today I am midway in a successful diplomatic career. The reason for this letter is my decision to put to work in the private sector the skills I have acquired. While I have the wide perspective of a generalist, I have exercised a specific discipline in re-establishing control over expenditures that threatened to get out of hand in two embassies. My knowledge of French and German is another concrete point of reference.

Putting these elements together, you may visualize me, as I do, potentially in a liaison role between headquarters and the field in an organization with holdings in sometimes 'difficult' countries.

In the hope that you may feel it would be useful to talk over our possible mutual interests, I would be glad to hear from you as to when such a meeting might be possible.

Yours sincerely,

This letter went out to 45 companies, the majority in the commodity business, with stakes in developing countries. It produced six meetings which in turn led to two good job offers. Ronald accepted one of them. He joined a worldwide commodity trading company headquartered in London. 'Commercial Ambassador' could well be the most descriptive title for his newly-created post. Less revealing but more dignified, his business card reads 'Co-ordinator of International Relations'.

SURPRISES ARE COMMON

Peter Peterson was director of research of an electrical engineering firm in Sussex grossing £100 million a year. He found himself out of a job at the age of 42 because his company was forced out of business. Peter had a degree from London Polytechnic; he liked working with electricity, but he was aware of having missed out by not getting into some form of electronics. Peter addressed a motivating letter to a variety of companies manufacturing a wide range of electrical products from generators to household equipment. Not only did he give specific examples of the results of his research, but also stressed his success in co-ordinating teams and steering his innovations through the manufacturing process. Without being specific, his letter strongly suggested that he was capable of assuming a larger role in the management of a technically oriented company.

His example is particularly interesting. It illustrates that the results from this kind of letter are often unpredictable. Among the handful of replies he generated was one that led to a meeting with the managing director of a decentralized group of electrical companies. At one site, they manufactured heating equipment, at another switchboards and in still other locations a range of other specialized projects. What was lacking, the managing director revealed, was any kind of co-ordination at the research level. There was duplication, he knew, but he also strongly suspected that opportunities for new developments were being missed due to a lack of synergy between the different units. Would Peter be interested discussing the job of synchronizing the various research activities that existed?

He was interested, but the conversation then took off in a new direction. The boss felt that the insertion of an outsider into the central management hierarchy might cause resentment in the field. From this and other standpoints it might be preferable to cast Peter in the role of outside consultant. The idea took form and today Peter is the proprietor of his own technical company. Peter had become an example of outsourcing — the most dynamic development yet in the rise of the service industry, which today comprises two-thirds of all business activity.

CREATIVITY EQUALS OPPORTUNITY

Perhaps the most radical change I have experienced is that represented by Samuel Smallwood. At 38 Sam was young to be headmaster of a grammar school in Yorkshire. But try as he might he could not peer into his own future without a certain dismay. Already he was becoming bored with school administration. Yet he knew that a move upward was unlikely to the point of impossibility. Upward? Where to? Sam's feeling that he was facing stagnation was one reason why he threw himself enthusiastically into developing a programme to integrate computers into classroom instruction. He was, in fact, one of the pioneers of this trend. The hardest part was to obtain the backing of the school authorities and with it the modest funds needed to launch a pilot programme.

The solution came from an American computer manufacturer who was enthusiastic about expanding into the educational market. Working together in developing the needed software, the headmaster and the company developed a good working relationship.

The ultimate result? Sam was invited to join the company as an interface (in reality, a full-time consultant) between the organization and the entire educational community. Sam accepted, but where the post would ultimately lead remained to be seen. Too adventurous to remain in an academic career, he was willing — despite my counsel, I should add — to take a risk.

GETTING IT RIGHT

The motivating letter is not an easy letter to write. To be avoided is anything that smacks of self-glorification or hard sell. The example shown in Roland Roe's case history represented a particular challenge. This was to deal with the fact that Roland's career was not the kind that produces concrete, measurable results. A head of finance might point to concrete results: the systems he or she installed processed 30 per cent more work while utilizing 25 fewer staff. Even simpler is the situation of a successful sales manager who can cite figures to testify to an ability to move merchandise.

Fundamental to a successful letter is, first of all, to observe two very clear rules.

Rule no 1: Letters rarely 'trickle up'. By this I mean that communications sent to people on or below the department head level stand a good chance of ending up either in a file or in the hands of the personnel department. The nature of their occupations means that they are not likely to be centres of communication within the organization. On the other hand, the offices of people on the general management level serve, in part, exactly as such centres. Presidents, chief operating officers and general managers have a panoramic view of their company's operations. Once you have 'hooked' (a word you will encounter more than once in this chapter) the interest of such a manager, he or she may not, of course, shoot back a positive reply. More likely, he or she will pass your letter to the head of the most appropriate activity — or to the personnel department. No matter who is the addressee, the fact that the message comes from 'upstairs' makes a difference.

Do you feel that it would be presumptious to aim so high? Then ask yourself whether or not you really represent an added value to the company. Since this book is not a manual for débutants, I assume that this is the case. Secondly, keep in mind that proactivity is a quality cherished by top managers. Corporate success is not fuelled by shrinking violets and a mincing approach is unlikely to open many doors.

Rule no 2: Never send a CV. That can come later if necessary. Presented as a part of your first approach, a résumé inevitably proclaims, 'I want a job'. This contradicts the basic principle that you are not asking for employment; rather, you are offering a valuable service. Translated into the most practical terms, consider what happens at the moment your letter arrives. No doubt it will be opened by a secretary or assistant. (Only wishful thinkers believe that the word 'Personal' or 'Confidential' will change that.) Once a CV comes into view, the secretary's automatic reflexes take over and seconds later your letter and CV are on their way to the personnel department. Then what? Most personnel people feel they are there to protect the executive row from job seekers. To 'screen out' rather than to screen people into interviews becomes second nature in the face of the avalanche of CVs they must confront.

Exceptions to every rule being the rule, let us assume that a letter with CV enclosed does actually reach the desk of someone well up in the hierarchy. Preoccupied by a multitude of matters, this executive inevitably asks him or herself, 'Is an investment of half an hour of my time talking with this person likely to be justified?' With this question in mind, his or her reading (or more likely, scanning) risks becoming a search for negatives. Wrong school. . .product experience not compatible . . .long period of unemployment. . .looks like a small-company person and, finally: 'Miss Jones, send this person one of your nice "thanks but no thanks" notes'. When this happens, the danger is clear; such a turn-down is final because the typical formal career résumé gives the reader enough information to justify a definitive 'no'.

Remember, you cannot be rejected for something you have not asked for — in this case a 'job'.

The hook

Your aim — and it cannot be stressed too often — is not to ask for a job; it is to offer a service. At this stage you are simply seeking to make contact. In order to do so it is essential to hook the interest of the other person.

One way to accomplish this is to base the start of your letter on the existence of some common ground between you and the recipient. Take, for example, the head of a company that has introduced a number of successful products in rapid succession. If your experience is in marketing consumer goods, you might, for example, start out as follows:

> Your repeated success in launching a series of innovative new products is impressive. I note particularly your increasing activity in the European market. This means that we share common ground since I am international marketing co-ordinator for a foreign-based company which has mounted ten new product launches in the past ten years.

Or, in the case of a purchasing director:

> Gathering components from a variety of sources, as your company does, is no doubt good economics. Suppose, nevertheless, you could realize a saving of 0.5 per cent on your total purchases without loss of quality. This has been my most recent mission, successfully carried out; I would like to share with you some techniques I have found useful.

These specimen openings illustrate three important principles. The first is that each one *puts the other person first*. It avoids the self-centred 'I-am-writing-to-you-because' approach. Like most of us, a person in command tends to find his or her own situation to be the most interesting of all, so let us put him or her first. The second principle is the establishment of a *community of interest* at the outset. In one case, this communality is marketing, in the other purchasing. The third principle is that both openings *arouse curiosity*. The addressee is likely to continue reading simply to have the answer to the question, 'What in the world is this all about?'.

The tug-along factor

The letter's ability to arouse curiosity at the outset illustrates a point that is important throughout the letter. Each paragraph must tug the reader into the succeeding paragraph. Assuming the purchasing director in the second example above, has tugged his or her target into the second paragraph, he or she says:

> These techniques I have come to group under the heading 'marketing-purchasing'. They are particularly applicable in special situations such as yours where you are sourcing in regions widely separated and far from home base.

Now the reader again scratches his or her head. 'What is this guy selling — some kind of consultancy service?' He or she must continue reading in order to have the answer. (Which, incidentally, may never be forthcoming in cases where the possibility of acting as an independent consultant might be an option for the writer. Keep in mind the sole object of the letter: to have a meeting — not, at this point, a job.) Thus the letter continues:

> No doubt you have your own guidelines covering purchasing and logistics. I feel that a meeting between us to explore our respective ideas could be a useful use of your time. But first, you may well be interested in having some background on my activities in a company that in certain markets is competitive with your own.

The proposal of a meeting always carries the risk of turning off the reader. Note in this case that the writer promptly reinjects the element of curiosity arousal by mentioning what seems to be a competitor.

Introducing yourself

His contact with the reader still maintained, our purchasing director at this point is in a position to sketch the major elements of his own background:

> One reason for my creative approach to purchasing is that I started out as a salesman with one of the world's top makers of office equipment. In such a job, sitting back to await the arrival of a buyer would be suicidal. I apply the same aggressive approach to purchasing. This means packing a suitcase and going into the field to seek out the best suppliers wherever in the world they may be. The figure of a 0.5 per cent cost reduction on all purchases is not at all imaginary; this is the result I am able to show after two years on the job.

To be noted in this paragraph are two vital points: (1) the use of concrete fact and the absence of boastful self-promoting adjectives, and (2) the frequent use of the present tense rather than the past. Why are the headlines in your daily newspaper in the present ('War breaks out' not 'War has broken out')? The reason is clear; the present sells more papers than the past.

The ending

Like certain composers of symphonic music, letter-writers sometimes seem to have trouble bringing their creation to a close. Few sign-offs are more clearly guaranteed to weaken a letter than those which cast the writer in the role of supplicant. Typical is: 'I look forward with pleasure to the opportunity of meeting with you.' While saying nothing, such phrases serve to put the writer in a position of inferiority. Because a good salesperson knows he or she must 'ask for the order', a stronger ending becomes:

> In order to explore further our interests in common, I suggest we meet. Please let me know of a time and date convenient to yourself.

SOME DOS AND DO NOTS

- Do not write a long letter.
- Do confine it to one page with comfortable margins.
- Do not try to write a sales letter.
- Do keep in mind that your objective is to get a meeting and that is all.
- Do not be egocentric, talking always about yourself.
- Do count the number of times you use the first person pronoun ('I', 'me') and the number of references to the second person ('you', 'yours'). Come as close as possible to a balance between the two.
- Do not focus on the past. The word 'experience' is meaningless; even a child has experience.

- Do talk about what you can do rather than what you have done — and in the most concrete terms possible. Remember always that the present is more interesting than the past.
- Do not end each paragraph with a completed thought.
- Do regard it as a way to lure the reader on to the following paragraph.
- Do not write long paragraphs. Busy people may have a short attention span.
- Do limit each paragraph to five or six lines.
- Do not end your letter as supplicant.
- Do close it in a businesslike way, stating clearly what you propose; namely, to meet the other person.

WORDS THAT WORK

Instead of saying 'I am *hoping*' for this or that — which is passive — it is better to say 'I am *seeking*. . .'. Sadly your 'hopes' are of little interest except perhaps to father, mother and wife, while 'seeking' something is proactive rather than passive.

In the same sense, it is better to be '*enthused*' by this or that than to '*like*' something. Again, the first is active, the second more passive.

Avoid any hint of pomposity. For example, instead of speaking of '*one*' or '*oneself*' it is better to use '*I*', '*we*' or '*you*' as the case may be.

Don't hesitate to employ common contractions such as '*I'll*' or '*wouldn't*'. They tend to take the stiffness out of your message.

When saying good things about yourself you risk seeming to boast. Rather than to declare '*I am very good*' (at such and such) it is better to say '*Others often remark*' (on my ability to do such and such).

'*My responsibilities include*' such and such notches up your level as compared with '*My job is to*' do so and so.

Beware of adjectives and adverbs. 'I am *interested* in. . .' is stronger than 'I am *very interested* in. . .'. Likewise, '*I am seeking*' such and such is more effective than '*I am actively seeking*' such and such.

Few candidates find a motivating letter easy to write. Perhaps that is because few attitudes are harder to achieve than objectivity about oneself. I recall one person who encountered such a block that for two months he was unable to produce a single sentence. Finally, impatient with himself, he came up with a letter. To his surprise, it turned out to be one of the most successful I can recall.

To reflect, to write and rewrite is the same process that goes on in advertising agencies and promotion departments where high stakes ride on finding just the right word and 'tone of voice'. For the person in a process of career change the stakes are even higher. They involve not only monetary rewards but the degree of job satisfaction he or she will have in the years to come. As a best-selling American author put it: 'inspiration is 90 per cent perspiration'.

THE LOOK

First impressions are just as important when you introduce yourself by mail as when you appear in present.

Chapter 5's discussion of the third-party letter to recruitancy professionals touches on this subject. In common between that letter and the motivating letter are the following recommendations:

1. Select stationery of superior quality.
2. Your name, address and phone and fax should be imprinted in businesslike, conservative characters.
3. Choose a lightly tinted paper so your letter can be identified readily in a pile of white documents.
4. Sign with blue-black ink, preferably with a fountain pen rather than a ball-point.
5. Avoid the use of window envelopes.

Whereas the third-party letter (see page 79) is most effectively addressed to the recruiting firm as a collectivity, this is of course not the case with the motivating letter. Each one must give the impression of being the only letter mailed. (While the recipient is not likely to be under this illusion, he or she is almost certainly going to be turned off by being the evident target of a mass mailing. In any case, when your letter is 'individualized' there is no hint of how many people you are addressing.) On this matter, here are points worthy of attention:

1. The recipient must be addressed by name and title — both on the envelope and at the start of the letter.
2. Never use address labels.
3. Never use a process that prints multiple copies of your letter, with the name and address of the recipient to be filled in afterwards. It is almost impossible to achieve a perfect match between the two portions of the letter, therefore it is immediately identifiable as one of a quantity being sent out.
4. Avoid the use of metering. Affix real stamps — and why not attractive commemorative issues?
5. If you are in a relatively visible job, especially within your own industry, you are perfectly entitled to write the word 'Personal' or 'Confidential' on the envelope. Junior executives, who do not yet represent such 'valuable property' should refrain.

Finally, a reminder: post your letters on a Monday or Tuesday to circumvent arrival on a Monday or a Friday — frequently days of distraction in the executive wing.

A 'numbers game'

Even before sending out any letters, whether they are third-party letters or motivating letters, you can have in hand a way to measure the success of your mailings. You should receive a total response, regardless of the quality of the replies, of 50 per cent or more.

The second measurement concerns the content of these responses. They are likely to fall neatly into three categories, as follows:

1. Positive replies.
2. Negative replies.
3. Maybes.

For purposes of record-keeping, I define a 'positive' reply as any response that calls for some kind of action on your part. The most encouraging of positive answers is, of course, 'please telephone me'. Two other calls for action, less likely to produce a concrete result, are 'please fill out the enclosed form' or 'send us a CV'.

Negative replies are easily identifiable because they communicate a firm — and probably irrevocable — 'no thanks'.

A 'maybe' response says, in effect, 'we will keep your letter on file for possible future action'.

To gauge whether or not your letters have 'hooked' the reader, it is the positive replies that count. Based on the experience of my clients, I suggest you take 10 per cent of replies as a benchmark. In other words, one out of ten of the letters you have mailed has produced a positive reply of one sort or another.

(Note: how to deal with each type of response will be discussed later in this chapter.)

THE FOLLOW-THROUGH

The best way to organize a follow-through system is to create two sets of three file folders — one set for the third-party letter; the other for the motivating letter — in which to store responses alphabetically. Mark one of the three folders 'positive replies' another 'negative replies' and the third 'maybe'.

Aside from categorizing your responses in this fashion, I also suggest you track them in terms of when they are received. To do so, set up a graph with vertical divisions representing the days of the month. Then enter each day the number of replies from each mailing. Typically, you will emerge with a bell curve showing relatively few early responses, then climbing to a peak before descending to a more-or-less extended period of flattened response.

Two or three weeks into the period of reduced frequency, you will be able to judge how effective your mailing has been. A percentage of positive responses that falls well below the 10 per cent figure I have proposed means that you have fallen short of your target. If the figure is substantially superior, you have reason to hope for one or more job offers.

'But 10 per cent of how many?'

This is a key point since it raises the question of the optimum size of a mailing. Someone once said 'averages never apply to anyone'. Nevertheless, based on the experience of others, we can calculate the minimum number of letters to be sent if you are to have reasonable assurance of a successful outcome. To do so, let us return to our benchmark figure of 10 per cent positive replies.

In general, one half of these 'positives' can be expected to result in a meeting with a company or recruiting firm. However, it is important to keep in mind that only one out of seven or eight meetings is likely to produce a firm job offer. Keeping our calculation simple, let us arbitrarily apply these ratios to an imagined total of 200 letters sent — 100 to recruiting firms, 100 directly to companies. Thus a typical result might be:

Letters dispatched	200
Total response (50%)	100
Total 'positives' (10% of total)	20
Total interviews (50% of 'positives')	10
Total job offers (1 out of 8 interviews)	1 plus

My credo is that ideally no job change should be made on the basis of only one concrete possibility. This means that a mailing of less than 200 letters is likely to produce a marginal result. The resulting shortfall from the ideal number of offers will be made up by other approaches, to be discussed later.

Some — perhaps most — candidates are taken aback on learning how much work a sound exploration for a new post requires. The fact is that one major reason for the unsatisfactory outcome of many job searches is the tendency of most people to think in terms of too small numbers. We know how much valuable experience we have to offer; we reflect on our winning personality and we naturally conclude that the world of work will welcome our arrival on the job market.

Simply put, realism at the start of a campaign is infinitely more useful than knowledge arrived at too late.

Enter the variables

Two factors can serve to modify this typical expectation. The first is the quality of the mailing itself — in terms of appearance, selection of targets and, above all, what the letters say and how they say it.

A second variable lies in the interpretation of results. Who signs the responses is important. If roughly half of the replies are signed by the person to whom your letter is addressed (or at least by another top operating officer) you can assume that your 'hook' has done its work. Letters signed by secretaries or personnel staff are not likely to bode well unless they are invitations to a further contact.

WAYS TO RESPOND. . .

. . .to positive replies

Among your positive responses (those proposing some action on your part) the ones asking that you make direct contact are the simplest with which to deal. Usually the purpose is to arrange a meeting. However, this is not always the case. Particularly if the person you are to call happens to be a personnel officer, a telephone contact can turn out to be nothing less than an interview by telephone. This is a moment to be on guard; the telephone is often a highly unsatisfactory means of communication. It offers little chance to gauge the reactions of the other person and very little opportunity to seize the initiative. Verbally, you are addressing a one-way mirror.

My recommendation is to sidestep being trapped into a telephone interview; instead, seek a meeting. One way to accomplish this is to stress that you prefer not to reply by telephone to questions about personal matters. (This response is particularly apt if questions about salary are being broached.) You would, however, be glad to provide any information the other person wishes in the course of a meeting. 'When might this be possible?' You are perfectly justified. Who, after all, really is this stranger who wants to delve into your life? This is not paranoia; it is simply a question of discretion.

If, on the other hand, the telephone contact is simply to set up a meeting, there is only one standard rule to follow: always repeat the time and date proposed in order to remove any possibility of misunderstanding.

'Positive' (but requesting more information)

Among your responses, two other kinds of action may be proposed. One asks you to send a CV. The other encloses a form to be filled out and returned.

'*Send a CV.*' Here we see clearly the advantage of starting your exploration with a motivating letter. Now you know the identity of the company at which your résumé is aimed. If you need further information on its products or services, a bit of research may prove useful. With this information in hand, you can proceed to make certain modifications to your résumé. The object, of course, is to stress those aspects of your background that relate as closely as possible to the mission of the company.

'Fill out the enclosed form.' An enormous amount of time can be wasted on this sometimes futile exercise. Some companies send application forms as a part of policy to all who write seeking a post. (Such elementary questions as 'Do you have a driver's licence?' are a give away.) As for the rest of the requests, keep in mind that they are simply seeking more information in an organized form. Remember, you have intentionally kept your motivating letter short in order to arouse curiosity. Now at least you have some evidence that you have succeeded in your purpose.

Nevertheless, returning an application form nearly always leads nowhere. Instead of investing a lot of time, fill out only the first page. There you usually find questions which are about your address, telephone number, schooling and such. Very likely the next section asks you to detail your job history — including salary. Instead of filling out all of these little boxes, simply paste the employment section of your CV on to these pages.

Where a list of references is requested, a simple statement, 'To be submitted later if required', will suffice.

Some forms clearly show traces of the work of a psychologist. 'What do you consider to be the major influences that have shaped your career?' In replying, three rules can be helpful:

1. be brief;
2. be positive; and
3. be optimistic.

For example: 'I have always enjoyed working with figures, so finance was a natural choice for me — and the right one judging from the steady upward progress shown in my CV.'

'Maybe some day'

Since no action is asked of you, the polite brush-off can hardly be categorized as a positive response to your letter.

However, all is not lost even when a company writes, more or less, as follows: 'We will retain your letter for consideration should future opportunities arise.'

Often a less-than-elegant translation of this bureaucratic wording might be: 'buzz off'. However, I suggest that you deliberately ignore this possibility, accepting the statement at face value. Let four or five weeks go by, then send your reply — this time enclosing a CV. Your message might go along the following lines:

> On (such and such a date) you kindly suggested that you were keeping my correspondence on file against possible future opportunities with your company.
>
> Since then I have created the enclosed CV which contains supplementary information about my background and qualifications. With the passage of time and in the light of this amplification, you may wish to follow up our contact at this time.
>
> I propose a meeting for this purpose and would be glad to know when this might be convenient to you.

The chances of success from this approach are not great. However, the letter is short, your CV has already been prepared and a postage stamp is not a major investment. So why not give it a try?

The pages that follow describe an entirely different approach to searching the market for your best future possibilities. We are about to examine ways to open doors to executive search firms — more often referred to as headhunters. The most highly regarded are usually to be found in Mayfair. They work for companies that pay them generous commissions for finding the 'right' person. The most august do not advertise openings in the press, although there are certain highly respectable exceptions.

Up to this point I have tried to make it clear that a fruitful exploration of the job market is not likely to be based on any one technique. Many of the most interesting and lucrative posts are to be found in the files of the professional search people. Despite their reputation for aloofness, their doors can be prised open by candidates — if approached correctly.

What do I mean by that? Read on.

5

Contacting the Pros

By 'pros', I mean all of the professional recruiters who help organizations to fill executive positions. In the western world they number in the thousands. However, it is important to note that the fraternity is divided into two categories.

Category 1 comprises the top of the breed, the 'headhunters' as they are known outside the profession (they themselves prefer to be called management consultants or executive search consultants). These firms rarely, if ever, advertise their searches for candidates. They find the 'heads' they are hunting by means of research, networking or reference to their files. If they are members of a recognized professional association, they are likely to be operating under a clearly stated code of conduct.

Directories listing the addresses of the major firms are available in almost every major developed country. The best way to obtain such lists for any country other than your own is likely to be by contacting your national chamber of commerce located in the foreign commercial capital. At home, any public or business library will help you. Such directories usually identify search firms that specialize in some particular type of personnel, such as financial people, or they may service a particular kind of industry or category of services.

Category 2 is a mixure that defies generalization. However, these companies do have one characteristic in common; unlike the executive search firms, they use advertisements in the press as a way to seek candidates for their clients. They are less expensive for a company to retain but the quality of their services can vary widely. A small fraction operate under standards as high as those that mark category 1 even though, under special circumstances, they will advertise positions they seek to fill.

After that, it is all downhill in terms of quality and efficacy. At the bottom are simply mail-drop services whose function is largely to protect the anonymity of client companies that are unwilling to be bothered by direct approaches from job seekers.

The non-advertisers. I have already said that trying to find a position by answering advertisements is perhaps the least efficient way of going about a job search. What follows, then, applies to the genuine executive search firms who do not advertise, plus a sprinkling of the best-known companies to be found in category 2. Let us be clear: approaching these top-drawer 'third parties' (so-called because they are neither the individual nor the future employer but an intermediary) becomes very much a numbers game. In fact, a starting list of 100 targets is likely to be minimal.

Why? Again we must look at numbers. Most people are surprised to learn how few searches are being conducted at any one time by a typical executive search firm. One of the best known is geared to handle about 100 per year in its New York office. This particular organization is unspecialized — meaning that this number includes a variety of executive categories, among them people in sales, finance and general management. Clearly, in this case, your mailing at any given time is likely to arrive when only four to seven searches are under way, and these for a variety of profiles. Even if your approach is well done, obviously the chances of clicking into a live possibility are likely to be small.

Only one logical solution exists. This is to increase the number of targets. Let us assume that a given firm is handling six searches at a time — probably about average. By contacting 100 firms, you are now in contact with 600 potential possibilities. Primitive thinking? To be sure, but there is no escaping the fact that any research designed to turn up the best positions available must be widespread.

Continuing to speak of numbers, I can usually predict that around 10 per cent of the letters mailed will, on average, result in interviews but that only one out of seven first interviews is likely to result in a concrete job offer. Either you find that the job is not for you or the search firm or the prospective employer does not see a good fit.

All such generalities are subject to a caveat: 'averages never seem to apply to any one'. It is evident that some profiles are more in demand than others. Nonetheless, it is possible to reason that 25 to 30 meetings resulting from approaches to professional recruiters combined with all other approaches will produce two to four solid propositions. This is, obviously, a minimum number if you are going to have a real choice of posts — in other words, a chance to select the best possibility available rather than simply to 'find a job'.

THE THIRD-PARTY LETTER

What is the best way to approach the pros? The following checklist will serve as a guide. First, however, let us be clear on one point. No method other than using the mail is likely to work. Forget trying to get through by telephone unless you know someone; you can be sure that every switchboard is protected by experts. To use the fax is simply a way to signal overeagerness, to say nothing of an evident brashness in tying up the other person's fax line. Since most of us, therefore, are condemned to use the mail, here are the elements of an effective letter to the people* I have referred to as 'third parties':

---

* For information about to whom to address your third-party letters, see the references listed in the Appendix.

The well-dressed mailing

Anyone who receives a quantity of mail soon develops some instinct for the status of the senders. Without thinking, the recipient links the quality of the paper with the quality of the person signing the letter. This means that saving a few pence on stationery simply serves to diminish your image from the start. (If advice is needed on exactly what kind of paper is most appropriate, get it from a quality printer specializing in personal and business letters.)

Using a lightly tinted paper (buff, grey or blue is not a bad idea) will serve to help make your letter stand out in what is otherwise a pile of white sheets.

Younger people just moving into management can get by simply by typing their name, address and telephone number at the top of their letter. For those already in middle management and up, I recommend the use of printed stationery that conveys an image of achievement. The use of engraving is rare today because of the development of satisfactory and less expensive processes. More important than the process is the character of type you select.

The typeface should be conservative without smacking of the 'nineteenth century' with its fancy swirls and loops. (Once again, a professional business printer of quality letters — not one of the instant print shops to be found today on nearly every street corner — can help with your choice.) Whether you choose to print just your address and telephone number or to start off with your name is of no importance. Depending on your choice, you will omit or add your typed name under your (perhaps illegible) signature.

A communication not an advertisement

The secret of a good letter is to set up a communication between the sender and the person addressed. In other words, it is not a kind of advertisement designed to tout your virtues.

One way to ensure a human touch is to use often the words 'you' and 'yours' rather than a constant repetition of 'I' and 'me'. To leave the other person out of your message is to set up a one-way communication from you to the recipient (in other words a non-communication).

Thus, 'Your organization may be acting on behalf of one or more companies seeking high-level financial managers such as myself', etc, rather than 'I am writing this letter because I am a top financial manager. . .'. Or again, 'Because of the international activity of your firm, you may be interested to know that I speak German and French fluently', instead of 'I speak German and French fluently'. 'Your location in Yorkshire is congenial to me because that is where I was born and raised', and not 'I grew up in Yorkshire'.

This effort to establish, to the extent possible, a person-to-person relationship is of central importance and will be the key later to achieving success in employment interviews.

The factor of time

Time is what a consultant in recruitment is selling. When we use rambling sentences, when we write by hand, when we repeat many elements that appear in an enclosed CV, we waste the other person's time and therefore his or her income. De Witt Wallace, the co-founder of *Reader's Digest* built his fortune on the principle that 'people do not take the time to write short'. Even though — as will probably be the case — you have to write and rewrite your letter several times to get it right, it must be an efficient communication. It should be couched in short sentences and short paragraphs, and it should use informal, everyday language rather than stilted, high-flown phrases. 'I look forward to hearing from you' is better than 'I shall anticipate eagerly the pleasure of receiving your response'. 'Don't hesitate to contact', instead of 'do not hesitate'; and similarly using 'we'll', 'here's', 'there's' etc. Of course contractions are shorter but they are also warmer and help to avoid stiffness.

Ideally occupying only one side of a single sheet of standard-size business stationery, the text, above all, should be logical in the progression and presentation of the subject matter. If so, the reader will be spared the need to study, rather than simply to read, your message. To achieve this kind of clarity, never be satisfied with your first draft. Put it aside for a day, then reread what you have done just as though you were the person receiving your letter. You will quickly see ways to improve your work, but even then two or three further revisions are likely to produce an improvement each time.

Expressing your own personality and way of thinking is paramount. That is why I am resisting the temptation to reproduce model letters as guides to the reader. Unconsciously or not, such 'models' almost always serve to warp one's own way of communicating. However, for use in your own way, here are some suggestions you might find helpful:

Begin with the words 'Dear Sirs'. To target a particular person inside a consulting firm is dangerous, even if that person is the chief executive. For the most part, recruiting organizations are a rather loose grouping of partners, each with a close knowledge of one or more sectors of activity. If you are not sure of reaching the person specializing in your particular industry or service, your letter risks ending up in a pigeonhole. You are better off using an impersonal greeting as your most direct entry into the firm's bank of candidates.

Keep in mind that you are not likely to have the good luck to come along just as the company is searching for someone of your profile. If not, it becomes important to ensure that your qualifications are fed directly into the firm's retrieval system for reference as the occasion arises.

The whole point of this particular kind of letter is to whet the other person's interest so that he or she will, out of curiosity, turn the page and read your résumé. To attract attention to your CV, you may want to point up certain highlights of your experience. However, to repeat in your letter the evolution of your career as set forth in the CV is a time-waster. Much more effective is to recount certain outstanding successes and accomplishments. Always avoid the word 'experience': a hollow and overused word. Even a child has 'experience'. The important question is what are the *results* of this experience?

The present versus the past. Why do the headlines in the newspapers nearly always use the present tense? Quite simply, because the immediacy of the present sells papers. The same principle applies in creating a good letter. 'I was this or that', 'I used to do this or that', 'I joined my company ten years ago' — all such historical statements tend to produce yawns. Wherever possible, write in the present tense. For example 'I am proficient in software design' rather than 'I learned software design', or 'I travel frequently' instead of 'I have travelled widely'. With practice, most people are surprised to learn how many past actions and situations can be described by the use of the present tense.

HOW TO CONSTRUCT YOUR LETTER

Here are some suggestions on how to create a letter that will open doors:

■ State why you are writing. 'Obvious, isn't it?' But an astonishing number of candidates launch right into their history without preamble. They fail to realize that the start is the place to establish a 'you and I' communication: in other words to make clear that there are *two* people in the equation not just one, yourself. '*Your* firm is well known as a recruiter of financial executives. I am writing to *you* because this is my profile and *you* may be interested in my availability.'

The italics, which will disappear in the letter, are there to make a point: the nearer you can balance your use of 'you' and 'yours' with the number of times you use 'I', 'me' and 'mine' the closer you will come to establishing a human communication rather than an 'advertisement' for yourself.

■ The time has now come to state your goals. This is tricky but necessary. The first challenge is to avoid being too specific. ('My goal is to be financial vice president of a medium-size company making brake shoes in Lincoln.') That way you can almost hear the doors slamming in your face. The second challenge is to avoid being so general that you appear to have no idea of who you are and what you want. ('I would like to take part in the management of a company with some international activity.') In speaking of possible job goals, it is important to use words that are neither overly precise nor too vague: 'I seek a post in the financial management of a medium-size manufacturer doing business transnationally' (not, 'I would like. . .'. Not only is this passivity at its worst, but the sad fact is that most people are not deeply concerned with our yearnings.)

■ This is the point to speak of your strong points. Major accomplishments are more important than titles, which in any case will appear in your CV. Accomplishments also can be quite specific, unlike the free-floating generalizations that weaken many letters. The following is very concrete: 'Faced with increasing losses that amounted to £5 million when I joined my company, I was largely responsible for turning around the situation. Four years later, we showed a pre-tax profit of £1,350,000'. (Note the precise figures; they serve to lend credibility to your statement.) To be sure, not every activity can produce quantifiable results. Taking macro-economics as an example, a bit of reflection might produce: 'macro-economic studies for which I am responsible were a major component of my company's short-term strategic forecasts which are running within 5 per cent of actual growth'.

■ At the same time, one has to keep in mind that figures are not people and that we are creating a communication between human beings. Who is this person who is writing the letter? Specifically what characteristics make him or her worth consideration? This brings us to the danger of seeming to appear to pat ourselves on our own back. How to state the truth that one is an excellent manager without bragging? A useful way out is to ascribe favourable remarks to others. For example, 'Over the years I find I have earned a reputation for. . . .' or, 'Repeatedly in executive evaluation meetings management recognizes that I am. . .'. Still again, 'Reference letters in the past have more than once commented on my effectiveness in. . .'. Since pinning medals on oneself is less than graceful, it makes sense to enlist, in some such manner, other people to do the job for you.

■ One matter that can be highlighted in your letter is your education, if it is impressive, along with any language skills you may have (to be featured prominently if you are targeting companies active internationally).

■ Are you flexible in terms of where you make your home? Say so. However, guard against writing a kind of blank cheque by giving the impression that you are poised to take flight at any time for any destination under any circumstances. The solution is simple: add 'for the right post' to any statement about your willingness to relocate.

■ To mention, or not to mention, your salary level? The answer is 'no' if you are either a junior executive or someone well up the hierarchy. In the first instance, an experienced recruiter will be able to guess how much you are worth. In the second case, top executives simply do not flaunt information about their remuneration. The professional searcher knows that the matter will be discussed once a clear fit is seen to exist between candidate and employer.

The salaries of middle-management people are, however, not so easy to divine according to title. Yet we must recognize the obvious: that because search firms exist in order to make money, the subject of salary level is of interest to them. Generally their revenues consist of fees based on a percentage of the winning candidate's annual salary. Thus the following equation becomes clear: with similar fixed costs, a successful recruitment of a person earning £100,000 per year will bring in half the fees realized through the placement of a £200,000 executive.

Here's how I recommend dealing with the matter:

— If you touch on the subject at all in your letter, mention your anticipated, rather than your actual, salary. (Normally this figure should be 15–20 per cent higher than your current level of pay. An increase of this order is a normal offset to the risk of making a change.)

— In calculating what you are being paid, be sure to take into account fringe benefits eg, medical insurance, use of a company car, executive dining-room privileges, life insurance and stock options. These should be reduced to an annual figure and then added to your base salary. (Always speak in annual, not monthly, terms.)

— Do not be arbitrary. Leave room for negotiation by generalizing your targeted pay. All that is needed at this point is to give the recruiter a ball-park idea. Using a rounded figure, speak of 'in the order of' such and such thousands per year. Alternatively you might say 'around' such and such a figure, or 'in the neighbourhood of'. Some people like to refer to a 'salary bracket'. The flaw in this approach is that the lower end of the scale is likely to be the choice of the ultimate employer.

■ How to close this kind of letter often seems to pose a problem. Why not take a tip from professional salespeople, say in the field of life insurance? At the point of closing a deal, they tend to be very precise: 'Sign here, please' they might say. 'Place your initials at the bottom of each page and write today's date in the space provided in the lower left-hand corner of the last page.' I suggest you employ a similar precision in ending your letter. Many an otherwise good letter has been weakened by a mushy ending, such as 'Hoping to hear from you soon' or 'I would be grateful to have the opportunity to discuss this matter with you'. (I prefer to think the receiver might be grateful to have a contact from someone as able as yourself!) In general, such words as 'hope' and 'gratitude' are worse than useless since they automatically place the writer in a position of pleader. Always remember, you are not 'looking for a job', you are proposing a service.

A much better close is to offer to supply any supplementary information desired. 'A meeting could be the best way to furnish you with any further information you may wish to have. Please let me know a date and time most convenient to yourself.'

Then that is it. You have proposed a clear course of action and any flowery words you might add will only serve to weaken your conclusion. All that is left is to add 'Sincerely yours. . .'.

CV OR NO CV?

No law states that you have to send a career résumé with your letter. In fact, if you are not conducting a search under time pressure, there is much to be said for a letter that stands on its own. If it succeeds in arousing the curiosity of the receiver, he or she may feel some frustration due to the absence of certain details. The solution is to seek more information from the sender and this is exactly the result to be hoped for. Such a request for more documentation may take one of three forms: 'Enclosed is an application form. Please fill it out and return'; 'Please send a CV'; or 'Please phone for an appointment'. The last is, of course, the happiest result but any of these responses can lead ultimately to a positive result. It goes without saying that this kind of two-step process is likely to take longer to flower than if you had provided more complete documentation at the start.

In any case, at some point in the course of your search, a CV is almost certain to be required. The next discussion will focus on creating the kind of CV most likely to carry you on to a successful result.

6

Creating a CV that Works

Ask 50 people how to create a good curriculum vitae and you are likely to have 50 different answers. This is not only confusing but it also can be stressful — unnecessarily so — because many people overemphasize the importance of the CV. To have on hand a well-organized written statement of your history and skills is of course sometimes essential and we will shortly discuss how to create such a document. What is troublesome is a kind of mystique that has come to surround the subject: 'If I can get just the right words down on paper in just the right form for a "CV", then my job-hunting problem is practically solved.'

Thus commercial CV-writing services abound and entire books are devoted to the subject, while other vital search activities may be neglected. Given the existence of such a fixation, it comes as no surprise that the CV itself is often seen as the cause of this or that rejection. Usually a period of tinkering and rewriting follows such disappointments in order to 'get it right', even though the 'rejections' were very likely traceable to some wholly unrelated factor.

Basically, one finds three types of CVs in circulation. I have come to refer to them as the 'traditional', the 'functional' and the 'pragmatic' models. You will find examples of each at the end of this chapter. They all have one factor in common: brevity. Keep in mind that for the reader time is money. You are saving his or her time when you yourself take the time to be as succinct and to-the-point as possible.

THE CV FOR EXECUTIVE RECRUITERS

Germanic employers may be alone in appreciating great sheaves of written information about a candidate. In other countries, generosity with details can become not only boring but dangerous. Most recruiters read a CV to 'screen out' rather than to 'screen in' candidates. Whether we like it or not, they feel they are being efficient when they economize on the time needed for interviews. The more detail you pile on top of detail the more likely you are to pass along bits of information that do not quite match up with the 'profile' of such and such a post. It is better to arouse curiosity through brevity than to suffocate the reader with unnecessary detail.

These thoughts hold particularly true in your contacts with executive search people. At the outset such people require only a one-page or, at the maximum, two-page snapshot of who you are and what you have been doing. With this information in hand, the reader can gauge quickly the degree of correspondence between the qualities you have to offer and the qualifications sought.

Now for a second generality. The interests of professional recruiters and personnel people are best served when you list your most recent activities first and then work backwards in your career history. What you have been doing lately is more pertinent than the job you held 20 years ago. This is the method used in creating a 'pragmatic' CV.

Some useful do nots

In Chapter 4 we opened our discussion of the motivating letter by clearing the air with a series of 'do nots'. Here then are the 'do nots' that apply to the creation of a sound CV:

■ Do not distribute handwritten CVs. No matter that you may be one of those rare people today who can produce elegant handwriting, the fact that business is business remains unchanged. Your résumé is a business document and should be approached as such.

■ Never send a photo. The reason employers in the US are enjoined from requesting one is that the practice is often racist or age-discriminatory. No matter how handsome or beautiful you are, you may be seen to be playing the same disagreeable game, but in reverse.

■ Do not use stationery with a printed letterhead for your CV. Instead, type atop the first page your name, address and telephone number plus fax and Internet numbers if applicable.

■ If you use word processing – and I hope you do because of its convenience – resist the temptation to create spectacular typographical effects. Lavish use of underlines, bold letters, capitals and changes of typeface tend to cheapen the appearance of a document and serve to diminish the status of the author.

■ Only under special circumstances use what is called a 'functional' presentation. By this is meant the organization of a CV by listing the skills and knowledge you possess rather than presenting a career history by dates. This format may be convenient if a number of more-or-less awkward moves have been made last in your career. However, the functional CV can pose a problem for the reader. At what point in the career was such and such a skill acquired? Evidently an experience in information management that took place ten years ago hardly has the same value as the same skill exercised currently. One way of getting around this difficulty is to accompany your inventory of skills with a chronology (as shown in Example 3 which follows).

■ Never touch on the question of salary earned or expected. You have the option of dealing with this matter in a covering letter, as discussed in Chapter 4. But keep in mind that the recruiter may want to send your CV along to his or her client; in other words, your potential employer. By separating the question of salary from your CV, you avoid hampering the recruiter in his or her negotiations on your behalf. Trust him or her; do not forget, the higher your pay, the higher is the commission earned by the recruiter.

■ Likewise, avoid listing the names of referees. If you have contacts with well-known people you may be tempted to bask in reflected glory. In actual fact, the reverse is likely to be the case. A premature list of referees says to the reader (correctly or not) that you need these people to support a lagging self-confidence. Even more practically, the risk of subjecting your referees to a number of unwelcome phone calls and letters is not to be overlooked. The proper time to deal with the question of references is in the final stage of a negotiation.

■ Until requested, do not submit copies of documents such as citations, diplomas and letters of reference. Let your background and the quality of your presentation speak for themselves.

■ While it may be convenient to list your office telephone number, resist the temptation. To do so is to send a signal that your company is ready to 'co-operate' in the matter of your departure. An exception to this rule is if you have a private office phone. In this case, give the number, but add the words 'direct (or 'private') line'. If you list the number of a home phone likely to be unguarded during the day, an answering machine becomes an excellent investment.

THE PRAGMATIC CV

The 'pragmatic' format is generally used by Americans. It is also preferred by executive search consultants everywhere because it is more convenient. (Also, perhaps, because professional executive search techniques originated in the US.) On the other hand, executive academicians and older, traditionally-minded companies may lean, if only by force of habit, towards a more classical CV arranged by chronology.

An X-ray of the construction of a pragmatic curriculum vitae follows:

Name
Address
Telephone(s)

PROFESSIONAL HISTORY
(Starting with most recent post)

Dates: from____ Name of company, location, brief description
     to ____ of company's activity

Your title: Responsible for (name major functions)_____
   from ____ _____
   to ____
            Major accomplishments _____
            _____
            _____

Title: from ____
   to ____ (THIS FORMAT TO BE REPEATED GOING
BACK TO EARLY CAREER)

EDUCATION
Name of institution(s), degree(s) and date
of degree(s)
Postgraduate courses such as company-paid
executive development courses
Languages and level of proficiency, spoken,
written

PERSONAL DATA
Nationality

Family situation

Possible mobility

OTHER ACTIVITIES
Name outside activities that are interesting
but non-professional

Professional history. Usually a person has held more than one post in the same company. In this case use the left-hand column to trace back each position, in reverse order as shown, leaving no gaps between dates. Give the most space to your most recent post, reducing the space with each backward move. This will produce visually an image of career growth. The words 'Responsible for. . .' are intended to lend weight to the activities to be described. Early in a career, however, there may have been no responsibilities. In which case, use the words 'Functions included. . .'.

Wherever possible add a brief summary of accomplishment, using figures to lend credibility. A sales manager might say: 'Increased sales 12 per cent despite a reduction of one-third in the size of the salesforce.'

Education. List only meaningful education, avoiding short-term in-house training. If language skills are highly developed and important in the post, *Languages* becomes a separate heading. In this case, it is useful to convey the level of your ability in each language, eg 'bilingual', 'fluent', 'read' and (if so) 'written'; or, at the lowest level of skill, 'working knowledge'.

Personal data. Skip age: 'Married, three children' suffices. If unmarried, separated or divorced, simply omit any reference to marital status rather than to stress the point. Especially if your target is to obtain an international post a mention of your mobility can help. Note then that you are 'Prepared to travel and/or relocate' or some similar wording.

Other activities. It is important to avoid time-wasting banalities such as 'likes music', 'jogging', 'omnivorous reader', etc. Work-related activities might be: fund-raising or golf for a sales manager, plus memberships in contact groups such as Kiwanis or Rotary. Avoid detailing memberships in purely social clubs or religious groups. Non-work-related conversation makers could include: parachuting, horticulture, archaeology.

Turn to the next pages for examples of the three basic types of CV:

1. *The traditional CV* — designed primarily to appeal to institutions (eg academic) and companies (eg publicly owned) to which respect for tradition may still be important.
2. *The functional CV* — intended to stress knowledge and capabilities rather than to trace year-by-year each career step. Perhaps there have been gaps between employers. Sometimes the problem is having made too many changes. Awkward also is the appearance of having made a step backwards in a recent career choice. The functional CV has gained acceptability with the demand today for 'knowledge workers' who offer expertise — though perhaps not acquired in the course of a 'typical' career.
3. *The pragmatic CV* — (as analysed above) preferred by professional recruiters and most management people.

The CVs shown here illustrate each of these formats. Note that each one is contained on one page. This is nearly always possible. Otherwise, consider two pages to be the absolute limit.

EXAMPLE 1: A 'TRADITIONAL' CV

Charles Cheltenham
1 Forest Close
Pinner MX HAS 2BN

Tel: 0181 868 0729

CURRICULUM VITAE

Personal information

Born 6 January 1955, in Birmingham. Two children, ages
4 and 6.

Education

Upper Birmingham Grammar School.
Manchester University, BA, Sociology (Hon 2), 1977
MBA, Henley, 1982.

Languages

Speaks adequate French. Some Welsh.

Career history

October 1977 to May 1979	*Universal Properties*, Estate Agents, Birmingham. Started as a trainee, then was made sales representative, showing prospective clients office accommodations for rent or sale.
May 1979 to Sept 1981	*Miracle Copying Machines, Ltd*, London, UK, headquarters of the world's 2nd largest manufacturer of copiers. Starting in sales, sold copiers to business establishments. *April 1980.* Named manager, North London district sales office.
Sept 1981 to June 1982	*Studied for MBA at Henley.*
June 1981 to present	*Interactive Computer Company plc*, London. US based manufacturer of compact computers. *September 1981.* Member, Technical-Commercial team to introduce US Interactive PCs to Great Britain. *June 1986.* Appointed sales manager, Southern England and Wales. In charge of 4 persons. *November 1990.* Commercial manager, England. Full responsibility all sales and marketing operations. *December 1992 to now.* General manager, continental Europe. Full responsibility for sales and marketing, 45 in staff. Introduced new models, Hummingbird and Rabbit PCs.

EXAMPLE 2: A 'FUNCTIONAL' CV

Charles Cheltenham
1 Forest Close
Pinner MX HAS 2BN

Tel: 01868 072911
Fax: 01868 753385

Education

Manchester University, BA in Sociology (Hon 2), 1955.
MBA, Henley, 1982.

Knowledge and skills

Successful international sales and marketing.
Strategic planning and implementation.
In-depth user knowledge of computer systems.
Launching in Europe of two new brands.
High-level contacts with major prospects and clients.
Effective management of a team.
Incentive and motivation of commercial personnel.
Direct sales of non-electronic equipment.
Recruitment of personnel and foreign distributors.
US management practices.
Business French, some Welsh.

Achievements

1981 — Named to 'Fast-Track Club' of top salespeople of Miracle Copiers Ltd, London.
1982 — Participant in small team of pioneers to introduce Interactive Computers of US into UK market. Profitable within one year.
1986 — Named regional manager, Southern England and Wales. Regional sales increased in three years from 50 million pounds to 80 million.
1990 — Named commercial manager, UK. Personally sold Interactives to Super-Eco and Everready — the two largest mail order houses in the UK — as well as Forcible Steel, Grandiose Electric and others. In two years UK sales increased 85 per cent.
1992 — Named general manager, continental Europe. Recruited 45 people, and agents with zero failure rate. Increased sales of original model plus introduction of two new Interactive brands (Hummingbird and Rabbit) resulted in a 450 per cent sales increase. Profit from continental operation jumped in three years by 63 per cent.

Personal

Married. Two children, ages 4 and 6. Prepared to travel and/or relocate.

EXAMPLE 3: A 'PRAGMATIC' CV

Charles Cheltenham
1 Forest Close
Pinner MX HAS 2BN

Tel: 0181 868 0729
Fax: 0181 753 3585

CAREER HISTORY

1982/now	*Interactive Computer Co plc, London.* *Headquarters of the European subsidiary of Interactive Computer Co, Inc, USA.*
1992/now	*General Manager, Continental Europe.* Responsible for all commercial and logistical operations in Western Europe.

> *Results:*
> Recruited and trained 45 technical-commercial people and office personnel.
> Selected, trained distributors in 6 nations.
> Increased territory sales by 450 per cent, partly through successful introduction of 2 new models (the Hummingbird and Rabbit PCs). Increase in net: 63 per cent.
> Negotiated office, assembly and storage sites with authorities and property agents in each country.

1990/92	*Commercial Manager, UK.* Responsible for the training and results of a sales team of 8 technical-commercial people.

> *Results:*
> Sales increased in two years by 85 per cent.
> Personally sold Interactives to 2 largest UK retail chains — Super-Eco and Everready as well as to Forcible Steel, Grandiose Electric and others.
> Outsourced after-sales service to cut overhead.

1986/90	*Sales manager, Southern England and Wales.*
1982/86	*Trainee, then member, technical-commercial team.* This group introduced Interactive PCs to Great Britain.
1981/82	*Completed studies for MBA, Henley.*
1979/81	*Miracle Copying Machine, Ltd, London.* (World's 2nd largest manufacturer of copiers.) *Manager, N. London sales office.* Sales trainee, then sales representative. Named to 'Fast-track club' of salespeople.
1977/79	*Universal Properties, Ltd, Birmingham.* Sales representative.

Education

Upper Birmingham Grammar School
Manchester University, BA, Sociology (Hon 2) 1977.
MBA, Henley, 1982.
Languages: speaks business French and some Welsh.

Personal

Married. Two children, ages 4 and 6. Prepared to travel and/or relocate.

7

Advertisements

The moment has come to look at the visible side of the job market: that is, those posts (and sometimes candidates) that are advertised publicly.

A part of this discussion — that having to do with an individual publicizing his or her own 'availability' — can be brief. Without exception, I have found self-advertising to be a waste of money. Faced with a client to whom cost is unimportant and who is determined to give advertising a try, I have an opportunity now and then to confirm this statement.

Two kinds of response to self-advertising are likely. The first is from employers who read such advertisements looking to pick up a good employee at bargain rates (reasoning that a person who resorts to advertising must be either naïve or desperate or both). The second kind of reply comes from people with something to sell. (From one self-advertisement in a newspaper with two million readers, the total harvest was one pitch from an insurance company and a second from a fee-collecting job-hunting service.)

APPEARANCES CAN DECEIVE

Before moving on to more promising actions, let us take time for a few more words of realism. I have already made clear that a search of the hidden, unadvertised job market is more likely to be fruitful than replying to notices of 'situations open' and 'appointments'. The reasons are evident. Representing barely one third of the jobs to be filled, advertisements attract virtually all of the competition in a highly competitive job market. Somewhere in a pile of hundreds of replies (a not unheard of figure) an employer is almost always likely to find a CV that more closely relates to the advertised cut-and-dried profile than does your own. (Unlike a possible result from a good motivating letter, you can forget any thought of a post eventually being formed around what you have to offer.)

A job or a mirage?

Even more discouraging is the fact that a certain percentage of the positions-open advertised are not, in fact, available at all. In the case of positions to be filled in the public sector and in education, for example, often no competition exists from the start. The administration in question almost always knows who will accede to such and such a post. Nevertheless, public policy requires that the position be publicized.

Less often openings announced by privately-owned companies also, in reality, may not exist. This is because the person responsible for determining who gets the job wishes to flaunt his or her objectivity. He or she has already decided that a certain person within the organization is the right one for the post — largely because of the existence of a 'good chemistry' between the two. He or she then selects a dozen or so applications from the flood of responses and perhaps even interviews a half-dozen candidates. This person can then deliver an Olympian decision to his or her superiors: 'After a thorough-going search outside our company, I find that the best qualified candidate of all is (my friend) Sparks in components marketing.'

It distresses me to talk with people who wonder just what shortcoming on their part caused them to be 'rejected' for a post for which they were well qualified. This unnecessary erosion of morale can be avoided through a realization that one cannot be rejected for an opportunity that in reality never existed.

Finally, what is being advertised? In reality is it a position that is open or is the advert really intended to flog the services of a recruiting firm? This question may seem mysterious until one looks behind the scenes. Let us assume that you are the proprietor of an organization helping companies to search for candidates (while offering them the convenience of hiding behind your logo and address). Obviously your name must be well known if you expect to have the number of corporate clients you need to succeed. The easiest and least expensive way to promote your fame is to insert regularly advertisements for posts that exist only in your own imagination. Your logo soon becomes recognized and you soon are seen to be a 'leader' in the field.

Read each advertisement carefully. Is the job description specific and clear or does it speak in generalities? Beware of such phraseology as 'Dynamic young company seeks ambitious people on the way up'. Or 'Wanted: young director seeking unlimited opportunity'. Or 'Attention: candidates for top management'. Save your energy for targets that offer more fact than fluff.

HOW TO DOUBLE YOUR SUCCESS RATE

So much for non-existent jobs. Happily, the bulk of advertisements do indeed treat with posts that really exist. In times of moderate economic activity, the average executive job seeker can expect to have to reply to around ten advertisements in order to obtain one job interview. Using the counsel that follows, he can reduce this ratio to five applications for each meeting. No magic is involved. In the first place, there is little to be gained by replying to any advert in which less than 80 per cent of the characteristics listed correspond to your own profile. In the second place, more care must be given to the way you reply.

Conventional wisdom has it that the 'right way' to reply to an advertisement is to send a CV, a covering letter and perhaps a photograph. In fact, similar demands appear at the bottom of many advertisements, often along with other, more detailed instructions on how to reply. Inevitably the result is an enormous quantity of look-alike job applications, devoid of character, personality or any serious effort to relate what the applicant has to offer with the kind of person the advertiser appears to be seeking.

What really goes on

'What is so wrong with that?' you may ask. After all, facts are facts and a CV is, above all, a factual document. The employer should be able to pluck out of such a document the pertinent elements. This flattering view of managers and professional recruiters may well reflect reality. More often than not, however, these people never even see the incoming replies. They just do not have time to ponder the details of each of hundreds of applications.

Instead, the task is usually off-loaded to administrative people. To them, the very wealth of talent the mail produces is assurance that a quick round-up of candidates for interviewing will produce a satisfactory final result. (Regrettably, some first screeners never do get to the bottom of the pile. Long before then, they have identified the 20 or so people they believe to be worth interviewing; the rest may go unread.)

Keep in mind that first screening of applications is basically dull paperwork. It is an act of kindness on your part to help this bored person recognize in an instant that your profile corresponds to the profile of the post to be filled. To begin correctly, you must visualize that he or she has at hand the job description of the post in question. It is a fair bet that this description was also the point of reference for the promotion department or agency that constructed the advertisement. Thus your objective is clear; it is to stick as closely as possible to the guidelines as published.

As you proceed, keep your target firmly in mind. It is not the chief executive officer or even the director of personnel.

Rather you are communicating with the first screener who is awash in letters and CVs.

- *Step 1*. Determine that the job is really one that you want and also that your qualifications make sense in the light of the information published. Since we are proposing a certain investment of energy and time, selectivity is in order.
- *Step 2*. With a coloured pen or marker, underline every word in the advertisement that reflects the characteristics that the company is seeking.
- *Step 3*. Create a letter that, line by line, traces the content of the advertisement.

Creating the letter

Step 3 requires explanation. Let us return then to my reference to the job description that began the whole process of hiring. Since the writer of the advertisement and the first screener very likely are relying on this profile in doing their job, why should you not be similarly respectful of its content? In other words, do not try to be original. Instead, follow the model diligently, treating each element step by step — and in the same order in which each appears.

The 'feedback method'

Exactly the same principle applies to the words you choose. No matter how elegant your use of the language might be, suppress the urge to flaunt your skills. Prefer always the choice of words that the advertiser found most useful. For example, the advertisement seeks a 'proactive manager' with 'strong leadership qualities'. If true, your reply states that you are a 'proactive manager'. Then in a few sentences you cite evidence from your history to establish that you have this quality. The same applies to 'strong leadership' and so on. In other words you are neither a 'result-getting manager' nor a 'born leader'. Rather, you are precisely — word for word —

the person the employer is seeking. Small wonder I call this the 'feedback method'.

The repetition of key words to spark an unconscious recognition on the part of the reader is only common sense. However, some people find parroting the words of the advertiser to be simplistic — in other words, an obvious ploy. The reader of such a letter is, however, unlikely to be as self-conscious of the repetition as the writer. In our eagerness to be 'creative' and 'original' (neither quality, incidentally, having been cited among those sought) we make composing the letter harder than it needs to be; and, at the same time, less effective.

Nevertheless, the feedback letter is not easy to create. It is a way of telling about yourself but in quite a different fashion from that represented by a canned CV. Basing your letter on the elements of most interest to the employer you are, in effect, constructing your own version of a CV. The result is bound to be a positive presentation of yourself. It eliminates extraneous facts and sidesteps possible negatives.

What if the advert contains so little information that you have no elements around which to construct a feedback letter. In such cases, there is a real possibility that the advertisement is either spurious or that it was lazily prepared. My advice is to turn your attention to more serious notices. If, however, you know the name of the company behind the text and it is one that interests you, send a shortened letter along with a CV tailored to that particular industry or service.

Where the feedback ends

Situations-open advertising generally falls into two categories: notices inserted directly by employers and those published by executive recruiting firms. Most, but not all, independent recruiting companies give stereotyped instructions on how the candidate should respond. 'Send CV, photo and state salary requirements' is a typical sign-off.

Many companies as well as some top professional recruiters are likely to be more enlightened. Aware that they are seeking people on an executive level, they treat the reader as an adult, inviting the individual to present him or herself in his or her own way. Thus the advert closes with, simply: 'Send us your candidature. . .', 'To apply, contact. . .' or 'Write to. . .'.

By leaving the choice open, the employer knows that he or she will immediately learn something about the candidate from the manner in which he or she chooses to reply. Obviously the feedback letter is well suited to this approach.

Certain advertisers will list a telephone number. Always take the bait. Giving a telephone number is one way the company (or recruiter) can identify the most highly motivated respondents. Often the result will be the reception of an application form in the mail. (See Chapter 4, p. 74 for suggestions on how to deal with such forms.)

One of the more creative London recruiters responds to a telephone enquiry by offering the caller a choice. Would he or she prefer to write a letter stating his or her credentials or would he or she prefer to receive an application form? For jobs in which proactivity is important, the request for a form can be seen as a reactive response.

In dialing the advertiser, there is a danger of being pulled into an interview by telephone, which is never desirable. However, this is unlikely; the person at the other end of the line is probably hard put simply to deal with the heavy volume of calls an advertisement can generate.

Where the feedback method ends is in dealing with the other category: those advertisements where very specific instructions are handed down. Even if requested, do not send an all-purpose CV. Do not enclose a photo. Make no mention of salary (unless it is to say something like, 'my salary level falls within the range normal for the type of responsibilities in question').

If you find these suggestions — particularly the withholding of a CV — unsettling, ask yourself what, in substance, is a CV? The answer is, a CV is what you conceive it to be. In the case at hand, the feedback letter substitutes for a CV. In doing so, it has the advantages of precision we have already cited. Even if an advertiser insists on a stereotyped CV, he or she will hesitate to eliminate any candidate who clearly has the right qualifications.

Finally, the demand for a photo often is racially motivated; as for the subject of salary, this can only be dealt with properly in a meeting. Let us not dignify these stipulations by going along with them.

When to mail your reply

We have already mentioned the large number of replies likely to be generated by a typical advertisement. Aware of this, the job searcher often rushes to the postbox in order to be among the first candidates to be considered. As in other aspects of job hunting, this perfectly natural reflex demands re-examination.

My recommendation is that you wait ten days before posting your reply. The reasons are that:

1. Nearly everyone reacts in the same way. This means that the flood of early responses is more likely to be scanned rather than studied.

2. An advertiser is sometimes so impressed by the number of replies that he 'overscreens' and rejects too readily. What he may be overlooking is that the best candidates are also searching actively in other directions. Among them are bound to be those who will accept other offers. Once the advertiser begins to realize he has overscreened, a later reply will receive more careful attention. It is clear that a reply which arrives in the mail along with only two or three others is bound to stand out.

3. Above all, keep in mind that executive selection is rarely a hasty process. A passage of two to three months is normal. Consequently, there is little to be gained and perhaps much to be lost by rushing off your reply. Far better is to take time to produce the best possible response.

Keeping track

Orderly record-keeping is just as important in tracing the result of your replies to advertisements as it is to third-party and motivating letters. The procedure in Chapter 4 for classifying responses to motivating letters works equally well in the case of replies to advertisements. There is, however, one important difference; you may have no opportunity to know the name of the company behind any given advertisement if it has been placed by an outside recruiter.

IN SUMMARY

Earlier I stressed that answering advertisements is likely to be less fruitful than making approaches to the non-publicized employment market. At this point, two amendments to that generalization are in order. The first is that the process of writing to advertisers is unambiguous; if you are invited for a meeting, your background obviously bears some relationship to a post that is open. If not, that is clearly the end of the matter. This open-and-shut nature of applying to advertisements means that you soon at least know where you stand. In contrast, replies from your spontaneous applications may suggest vaguely that you will be kept 'on file for future reference'.

The second important modification of my wary attitude towards advertisements has to do with the method used by the candidate. Based on my experience with my clients, I am convinced that certain people could reply to advertisements for the rest of their life without having even one interview with a prospective employer. As examples, I think of two such people, each of whom had sent off, without result, more than 100 applications for advertised posts. Since they both had good qualifications, the trouble appeared to be one of method. This was soon confirmed: once they started to follow the guidelines I have outlined here the pattern promptly changed and they began to have meetings.

Are there other ways of opening doors than those discussed up to this point? Indeed there are: for example, the chain letter which we will examine next.

8

Networking 1 — The Chain Letter

To repeat, a well-conducted search for the right post at first seeks contacts rather than a job. This is not word-play as can testify thousands of job seekers who have burned up their possibilities at the start. Among them are those who have fired off CVs to all of the companies that constitute their best targets; and without result, for reasons we have examined.

Another critical phase is the matter of approaching friends and business contacts. The person who has been 'let go', for whatever reason, is particularly prone to making a misstep. Frequently such people find themselves in a state of shock. 'How could this happen to *me*?' is often the reaction. Sooner or later it becomes clear that 'this' has indeed happened and that it is time to act constructively. Then may come a deceptively soothing thought: 'Think of all the people I've known in the past years — some of them well connected. Surely one of them will help me land on my feet.'

Such optimism seems fully justified by what comes next. The job seeker meets with X, has drinks with Y and lunches with Z. It is all very agreeable, but six months later, comes disillusionment; nothing has happened. More than a return to square one, the candidate now finds him or herself back at square minus one. On top of the first reaction, 'How could this happen to me?' comes a second, even more depressing thought: 'No one seems ready to lend me a helping hand. No one really cares.'

The reason for this frequent impasse is not hard to find; the person has been asking for something impossible to obtain. In fact, most managers are chary of bringing friends into their enterprise. Aside from possible accusations of nepotism, there is a real risk of damage to the existing friendship. This is due to the difference between the way people relate to each other inside and outside a work setting. I can cite too many situations where grave damage has been done both to a friendship and to a career because this difference has been overlooked.

To avoid this danger, the person contacted may well proffer an introduction to someone he or she knows. Such meetings almost always turn out to be encouraging. Very likely this friend of your friend will be cordial, maybe even asking for copies of your CV to show to others. Here again, unfortunately, the situation is not what it appears to be. For a reason evident to an objective observer, any concrete follow-through is unlikely. The sad fact is that the hospitality this person displays is not the result either of any particular merit of one's own or of deep well-springs of charity on the part of your host. Rather his or her welcome is rooted in a wish to accommodate his or her friend, the person who made the introduction. As a result, any real follow-through is unlikely.

Do these glum thoughts mean that any effort to establish contacts is a waste of time? Not at all. The challenge is to do so in a more effective fashion. One good way to accomplish this is to involve others directly — rather than at arm's-length — in your search.

The vehicle for doing so is what I call the 'chain letter'. Most people enjoy giving advice, and the chain letter takes advantage of this trait. It is designed to focus another person's thoughts on a very specific topic — the creation of your CV. Here is a subject on which nearly everyone is likely to have some ideas. In addition, a person outside one's own situation is certain to bring to bear far more objectivity than is possible for the author. However, as will be apparent, the request for a critique is only step 1 in what should become a chain of actions. How this happens becomes readily apparent in the following suggested outline of a typical chain letter.

CONSTRUCTING THE LETTER

A typical chain letter might go like this:

- Your (meaning yourself) experience in changing companies is limited due to your stable professional history.
- You are, however, certain of one thing — that you will need the best curriculum vitae you can create.
- Because of the other person's business — or professional — background and because he or she possesses an objectivity naturally greater than your own, you would welcome any suggestions for improvement of the draft CV you are enclosing.
- Since you are in contact once more, the thought occurs to you that your friend could well know of certain people who might be interested in receiving the final version of the CV. You would be grateful to have any such names and addresses and will not fail to mail copies to them.
- The close is a warm, personal sign off.

How slavish are you going to be when incorporating into your CV the suggestions you receive? Evidently, in each case, this becomes a matter of judgement. Frequently big and little suggestions of real value are proffered. Sometimes the simple omission of a fact might be noted. But I recall at least one occasion when a friend's suggestion resulted in a complete revision of a CV.

What is almost certain is that 20 people will have 20 differing views on how to present oneself on paper. You should weigh all suggestions in the light of the recommendations in Chapter 6.

As for the second letter — to go with your CV to the people suggested in the responses to your first letter — it might go like this:

> At the suggestion of our mutual friend, David Williams, I am sending you the enclosed copy of my career history. David thought that it might interest you — and that it might even correspond to certain situations you know about.
>
> Whether or not this is the case, I would be grateful to have from you the names and addresses of any persons you feel might like to receive a copy of the enclosed.
>
> (Warm ending.)

Being a consultant means that you are inevitably learning as well as counselling. One person with whom I worked found an original solution to a particular problem sometimes raised by the chain letter. He was troubled by the fact that contacting certain people by mail seemed stiff and unfriendly. So he arranged meetings in the course of which he outlined the chain letter idea. Did such an approach make sense to his interlocutor? As the conversation progressed, he found he nearly always received suggestions for his CV and the names of some people to whom to address it.

(This story illustrates a fundamental point. Every candidate is an individual with his or her own unique needs and situation. Whatever suggestions I make should be modified in any way that makes him or her feel at ease in conducting his or her search.)

OUTWARD BOUND?

An ideal target for a chain letter is the person situated in a foreign country where you would like to work. Your contact there might be either a citizen of that nation or an expatriate who is posted there. The important point is that he is in a position to know how things are done. In addressing such people your request for advice can be very specific, for example:

> I am attracted by the possibility of working in (name of country). Enclosed you will find a CV I have worked up for use here at home, but I realize that practices differ from country to country. Any advice you can give me for adapting my approach to your country (or the country where you are working) will be gratefully received.

> You can imagine also that I'd very much welcome having the names of people you may know there who you feel it would make sense for me to approach.

> (Friendly ending.)

TAKE TIME TO REFLECT

You know too few people to make worthwhile the chain letter approach? Think again. More often than not, this first reaction is the one I hear. Yet time and again I find that most of us have more friends and contacts than we realize. Sometimes a holiday card list or a list of telephone numbers helps to jog the memory. Also it helps to think widely. Even that neighbour over the garden fence might be someone worth approaching.

Another possible roadblock in the way of adopting this idea can be a feeling that people will be put off because you are 'asking for their help'. This idea, too, deserves re-examination. In fact, most people enjoy being cast in an agreeably authoritative role. They are likely to be flattered that you are enlisting them as accomplices in your search rather than as spectators (which is what the usual contact, in a vain hope that they will offer you a job, usually amounts to).

These two considerations — being open to enlarging your network and while enlisting others actively in your search — are at the heart of still another door-opener: the advice visit.

9

Networking 2 — The Advice Visit

Asking another person for advice is a no-risk activity whereas asking for a job, with negative results, can close doors.

The chain letter discussed in the last chapter is one way to make use of this principle. Proposing an advice visit is another way. To be avoided, however, is any intimation that you wish to cast the other person in the role of a career counseller. The importance of this basic rule will quickly become apparent.

But first, let us eliminate any lurking thought that this kind of meeting is some tricky way to try to snare a job. For the process to go well, your motive has to be clear; it is to seek a better understanding of the activity of which the other person is a part. To give intelligent answers, this person must be highly enough placed to have a rounded view of conditions within his or her industry or service. In other words, he or she holds a key position in general management.

The main objective of an advice visit is to compare reality with reality. In other words, to help you gauge whether or not there exists a potential fit between your own background and the needs of the other person's kind of enterprise. Even if it turns out that the two mesh well, the fact remains that 'asking for a job' has no place in such a meeting.

Why would a busy executive agree to a meeting in which he or she is expected to proffer advice? A look beneath the surface helps to explain:

■ First and foremost, most people love to talk about themselves and their job.

■ Second, unlike a job interview, this is a relaxed meeting with one person, the host, comfortably in the role of authority.

■ Third and not least, more people than we may realize are glad to be of some help to others. This is particularly true when a restricted investment of time is the only cost involved.

WHOM TO CONTACT

You do not have to know the person you will approach. In fact, I favour addressing complete strangers. Their motivation is clear; they freely choose to see you. No feeling of obligation is involved, as is bound to be the case when friendship comes into play.

Nevertheless, it is helpful to have some element in common with the other person. Perhaps you are graduates of the same school or you are fellow members of a club or association. Such links help to obtain meetings, though they are not completely necessary.

What is central to the success of this approach is your level of interest in the other person's sector of activity. Take, for example, the electronics industry. You are not an electrical engineer, but you have a sophisticated computer at home and at work and you are an avid reader of new developments in the field. Your sales and marketing experience lies outside the industry (which it must, or obviously you would have no need for advice). Nonetheless, you are wondering, at a time of career change, if it makes any sense to direct your search among electronics companies.

Most people are attracted by certain businesses other than the one they are in. If you have no such leanings, you would be well-advised not to undertake advice visits. Genuine interest in what the other person is saying either exists or it does not. If not, its absence is sure to be sensed by your interlocutor. You risk being seen as a fake.

In terms of how to make contact in order to set up a meeting, a good letter is likely to be the most productive method. Contact by telephone is an alternative but only if, first, you have mastered the techniques of breaking through the secretarial barrier and, second, you are unusually convincing once through.

CREATING THE LETTER

The opening. Your first order of business is to state why you are writing. Be clear on this point. You are asking for a maximum of 20 minutes of the other person's time.

The bridge. Faced with such a brief opening, the addressee is almost obliged to read on in order to learn why you wish to meet. This process of luring the reader on by arousing his or her curiosity must continue. For example, you might explain your request by stating that you are seeking the other person's advice on a matter that is partly personal, partly professional.

Clarification. This being a bit mysterious, most people will go on reading in order to have an explanation. The words you choose will be your own, but the sense of your message is:

1. You are in the process of reorienting your career.
2. You have an intense interest in the sector of activity in which the addressee is playing a key role.
3. Because of his or her position of authority in the field, he or she is in possession of the answers to certain questions you are putting to yourself.
4. Then, without delay, comes a disclaimer. It is absolutely necessary for you to state — and to mean it — that you are

in no way pitching for a job. Precise wording here is important because, in fact, you are obviously engaged in a search for a new situation. The essential point to make is that you are not targeting this person's company.

5. The moment has come to introduce yourself — but briefly. Without any 'selling', state who you are and what you have been doing in not more than two or three sentences.

The close. This letter is unique in that I suggest a follow-through by telephone: 'In order to facilitate our contact, I will plan to telephone you in one week to arrange a time and date convenient to yourself.' Do not propose contacting his or her secretary or 'office'; this simply serves to reduce your stature.

THE MEETING

The following steps are likely to characterize an advice visit:

■ The other person may be sceptical about the 'real' reason for the meeting. He or she has to be reassured that your sole purpose is to obtain his or her thoughts as to the possible fit between what you can do and the needs of the industry (again, not that particular company).

■ You will necessarily have to talk about yourself and your background. To help organize your thoughts, I suggest that you write out a short biography in advance — not, of course, to be read in the meeting — restricting the time of your recital to five minutes. Start with the present and work backwards. If you begin at the beginning, the interruptions and digressions may mean that you never get to the all-important present. A special word of warning: never take a CV into the meeting. With the other person's attention diverted to a piece of paper, a real exchange becomes unlikely. An even more important reason comes next.

■ Your host may ask questions, but in the end is almost obliged to make some kind of judgement. It might be negative. For example, in the case of a visit by a person hoping to break into computing, the host might conclude that his or her visitor's technical knowledge is simply too light. In this event you should ask for suggestions on alternative paths. You are also free to request the names of people you might contact in such sectors.

On the other hand, if the response is more encouraging, you can say that you are creating a CV based on your researches. Would he or she like to have his or her name added to your distribution list? Since his or her competitors would otherwise be receiving the CV but not him or herself, the response is almost bound to be yes.

Now you can see why I sometimes describe the advice visit as a 'cannot lose' transaction.

Another cannot lose door-opener, seldom thought of but capable of producing astonishing results, involves a special way of reading items that appear in the press. This is the subject of the next chapter.

10

Seen in the Press

News of change is the daily fare of newspapers and other periodicals. Among the changes they regularly report on are those taking place within companies. Some of these developments are 'bad news': declining figures, closures, bankruptcies. But a large number are of a more positive nature. These include announcements of new products, of promotions of key people, of executives on the move from one company to another.

From long habit, most of us tend to read these news items for information: in order to know what is going on. This is useful, of course; keeping in touch fuels conversation and updates our stock of useful information.

However, there is another way of reading such articles. It is a way that is especially applicable when we ourselves are in the process of — or at least contemplating — a change in our own situation. At such times I suggest you read with one question uppermost in mind — 'What's in it for me?'

Is this a bluntly selfish way of putting it? Obviously. Your situation demands that you make use of any and all information likely to help in bringing about a positive change in your situation. In the long run this may not be so selfish after all; the right next step can mean that you will go on to make a maximum contribution to the wellbeing of some enterprise and the people within it. 'Charity begins at home' is a phrase found not only in the English language. Its real meaning, of course, assumes that we must attend to our own needs if we are to fulfil the needs of others.

Here are some of the kinds of published reports that might have consequences for you:

- A company announces a new product or products. For example, a new line of men's toiletries.
- A foreign company reveals a plan to establish a subsidiary in your country.
- A board of directors names a new chief executive officer, or other major management changes are announced.
- A privately-held company plans to sell shares to the public in order to finance a programme of acquisition.
- A key executive makes an interesting speech or is interviewed.
- A company that suddenly begins to insert situations-open advertisements for a spectrum of jobs at different levels.

NEW PRODUCT

The company that announces a new product. You have a good track record in the sales and/or the marketing of consumer products. You see a big potential for the new product (or line of products). Here is an ideal moment to address a motivating letter to the chief executive officer. As stated in Chapter 4, such a letter must make clear the parallel between your activities and those of the company to which you are writing. In this case, your task is made easier by having access to the information published in the article.

COMPANY ACTIVITIES IN THE AREA

The foreign-based company that plans new or expanded activities in your area. If you happen to speak the language of the mother company, you have good reason to contact headquarters by letter. To staff up a new foreign operation, the company has two choices: to transfer existing personnel or to engage people already on the scene. Except for certain countries such as Japan (which invariably sends its own people overseas), you may have an advantage over candidates from the home office. Aside from your dual language capability, you know how things are done locally. Moreover, you represent an important saving; the usual compensation package, for example, for an American expatriate adds to the base salary a housing allowance, a car, annual round trips home and an educational allowance. Because America taxes its citizens wherever they are, a tax equalization scheme is also likely to be included.

Aside from the fact that you are a 'good buy', companies that name locals to responsible posts have found this to be good public relations. It enables the company to preserve a low profile against the more chavinistic elements in the host country and gives the staff hope that they, too, might be named to more important posts.

Finally, many overseas assignments end in disaster. Usually this is because the marriage partner is not happy in the new situation — a danger obviated by engaging people on the scene.

These selling points are not, of course, a part of your letter of contact. However, they might come in handy later on.

NEW MANAGING DIRECTOR

A new managing director is named. The last thing an incoming executive officer needs is unrest in the ranks. That is why he or she so often tells the staff to expect no revolutions. All will remain securely in their jobs and the avenue to the future will be evolutionary. Thus begins a honeymoon period which the new chief uses to get the feel of the situation, to size up the key people he or she has inherited and to refine his or her plans for the future.

(A notable example of this soothing, nothing-will-change approach was reported when the Dutch took over Baring's

Bank in the wake of a collapse that shook the financial world. Four months later the storm broke and dozens of high-level people found themselves out of a job.)

The honeymoon period is an excellent time to write to the new boss. Hampered by the need for confidentiality, he or she is unlikely to launch immediately on a search for new people. A spontaneous letter from an apparently able person is likely to receive more than routine attention. If his or her interest is aroused, he or she may propose a meeting, but with the standard caveat proclaiming the 'absence of any concrete possibilities'.

There is, of course, a difference in situation between a managing director who has been promoted from within the company and one who has been brought in from outside. The former has less need of an orientation period and indeed may know very well the composition of his or her future team.

SHARES GO ON MARKET

The private company puts shares on the market. In other words, new capital is coming into the organization. Unless the ownership is simply cashing in for purposes of self-enrichment, an influx of liquidity is likely to be destined to fuel expansion and improvements. The merit of making contact at this time is evident. Your motivating letter may well arrive at a time when new ventures are still in the planning stage.

EXECUTIVE INTERVIEWED

A key executive makes an interesting speech or is interviewed. Is the speaker active in a sector of activity that attracts you? Does what he or she says jibe well with your own ideas? If the answers to both questions are 'yes' you have a potential point of contact. The first step is to prepare a letter telling of your appreciation of the points made by the speaker and stressing the similarity between his or her ideas and your own.

Even (or perhaps especially) people of undisputed accomplishment respond well to expressions of appreciation from others. A client of mine of Italian origin provides a good example. Based in London, he read an interview in a business magazine with the head of one of Italy's largest industrial complexes. A short letter to the president must have struck the right note since the secretary wrote back suggesting the writer make contact when next in Milan. Though my client did not see the president, who was 'occupied', he was received by the human relations director. Some time after his return to London he received another letter — this time inviting him to send a CV for consideration for a post that was opening up (and which, ultimately, he turned down for valid reasons; nonetheless, the value of this method of contact was clearly established).

I can cite numerous occasions when this kind of approach opened doors. One marketing person read in the radio programmes that the president of a major food distributor was scheduled to speak. The person made a recording of the talk, played it back three or four times, and then wrote a letter quoting word for word certain of the most telling phrases. Not only was he invited to meet the executive but was received on a Sunday evening in his home.

You are right if you view such results as exceptional. However, the technique has a quality in common with others I have cited: it is one more approach where you have nothing to lose.

COMPANY REQUIRES HELP

The company that is advertising for help. A faithful reading of personnel advertising can yield rewards unconnected with identifying specific job targets. On occasion you might note that a certain company is publishing a number of situations-wanted advertisements covering a variety of posts. While these may be of a routine nature, this is no reason for you to flip the page. Clearly something is going on. One hypothesis is that wholesale defections have decimated the staff. Far more likely, however, is the possibility that the organization is in the throes of expansion.

The process of staffing-up may well reveal to the management the need for reinforcement of the executive team. This is an excellent occasion to send a motivating letter to the chief executive officer. There is no need to refer to the increased advertising, but the start of your letter might well speak of the 'problems often posed by expansion'.

Well carried out, the ways so far proposed to make contact with companies are bound to result in meetings. The question then arises, 'What kinds of presentation materials should I take into job interviews?' Too much and too detailed documentation can interfere with a good verbal communication. Too little may give the impression that you have not prepared adequately for the meeting.

For guidance on this important matter, turn to the next chapter.

11

Documentation

'Do you have a CV to show me?' is a standard query, particularly at the start of an interview prompted by a motivating letter.

This innocent question should ring more alarm bells than it usually does. Communication is impossible while the other person's attention is focused on a sheet of paper; furthermore, he or she may be all too prone to focus on points of vulnerability, putting his or her visitor on the defensive at the start of the interview. On the other hand, an apology for the absence of a CV does not promise to launch the meeting on a very positive note.

The most useful response is one that falls between the two extremes. 'I am in the process of preparing my CV. Would you like me to mail you a copy? Meanwhile, I can, if you wish, summarize the main steps in my career.' The response to your question and your suggestion is likely to be affirmative.

However, let us shift quickly from what documentation not to bring with you in order to examine the kind of presentation materials that can be useful.

For people in activities where the visual aspects of their profession are paramount, the matter is readily resolved. Architects, advertising people, interior designers, for example, are virtually obliged to arrive armed with a scrapbook showing their work.

Other executives, however, fail to consider that they, too, can use a portfolio to impart a (sometimes-needed) change of pace to their interviews. I am referring here not only to a switch from verbal to visual communication, but also to the possibility of moving the discussion on to a less formal level. To do so supposes the use of something more than a technical presentation. Rather it puts the focus on what newspaper people refer to as 'human interest'. They find it essential to introduce interesting items about what is happening to people in order to liven up their pages.

PORTFOLIO

The best-kept secret

Most job interviews rarely stray from the pragmatic. This is, in a way, unfortunate since an array of coldly factual data is not always the best lubricant for establishing a good rapport between people. Too often, we forget an important fact: people hire people. Either a current of mutual understanding passes between candidate and prospective employer or there is little hope of a positive outcome.

Is this the best-kept secret in the entire process of recruitment? If so, the reason is not hard to find. No recruiter gives as his or her reason for a favourable judgement the all-too simple explanation: 'I liked the chap. Some kind of current passes between us.' Instead, a process of intellectualization automatically takes over in order to produce more hard-headed, pragmatic reasons for the choice.

Thus the purpose of mixing personal and businesslike documentation is to bring a degree of warmth into the interview. At the highest levels of hiring, the idea of a portfolio may not be appropriate, but for middle managers and below such a scrapbook can be an extremely helpful tool.

But first, what kinds of items can usefully be a part of such a presentation?

The contents

The kind of portfolio I find most helpful highlights personal history. Instead of a volume crammed with graphs and statistics (though these might be present in limited quantity) I am suggesting that you offer insights into the kinds of activities that are not likely to be part of a CV. Two or three photos of your family — perhaps even of your home — are typical. Citations for good performance on and off the job speak louder than words. Photos snapped in the course of a speech and newspaper clippings mentioning yourself are typical ingredients. Other good items for inclusion are photos taken on the golf course, at the helm or engaged in other sporting activities.

If you include technical material, be sure that it is understandable to people outside your speciality. Keep in mind that most recruiters are neither engineers nor technicians. To ask such people to appreciate bytes and online multimedia risks dragging them across the threshhold of boredom.

Certain kinds of business documents are, on the other hand, universally understood. These include those showing:

- Sales increases.
- Increases in market share.
- Improved profit margins.
- Patents held.
- Involvement in foreign markets.
- Your place in the organization chart.

Most of us have collected — or are able to create — far more testimonies from our past than we realize. Sometimes a search through forgotten albums is necessary in order to rediscover such items. Occasionally one's partner can be helpful in ferreting out such items.

Involving the other person

Equally important is the question of how to prompt your interlocutor to examine the contents of a your presentation.

No action is likely to be less productive than thrusting a scrapbook onto others. As with any of your possessions, it should not even be placed on the desk of the interviewer (which can be felt as an invasion of his or her territory) but on the floor within ready reach. While out of sight, the portfolio should never be out of mind. As each topic of conversation arises, consider whether or not you have in its pages material that relates to what is being said.

Almost always, the talk will touch on some kind of relevant activity. For example, the interviewer of a purchasing manager might ask for evidence of the success of his cost-reduction programme. This is the moment to make the connection: 'I have with me some visual material on the subject that might interest you.' It is then that the scrapbook can be introduced in a very appropriate fashion.

After that, let human nature take over. Almost certainly the other person will be lured by curiosity into leafing through other pages. It is equally likely that he or she will pause here and there to comment or to ask questions. At no point can his or her attention be forced, but once interest has been aroused by some specific item, a discussion is bound to follow. Normally one subject will then lead naturally to another.

What happens in the unlikely event that no part of the interview touches on the content of your portfolio? In this case, you simply depart with the book unopened, counting on better luck next time.

THE FOLLOW-THROUGH

Well executed, the programme of action in this book will produce an important number of first meetings. Herein lies a danger. You will no doubt emerge from each interview with a clear memory of what was said on both sides of the desk. You may even be turning over in your mind how you might have handled certain questions differently. In short, every conversation is etched. . .until the next meeting. . .and the one after that. Unless you take preventive action, you will soon find it all too easy to mix up elements of one meeting with another.

Any such confusion poses a risk when you are called back for second meetings. The process of groping for what was previously said can inject an element of uncertainty into any exchange.

The best solution is to write an *aide-mémoire* recording the main elements of each conversation. I strongly recommend that this be done before the day ends. A point here and a point there can quickly melt into oblivion with the passage of hours.

To simplify this chore you will find it useful to create a checklist, make copies and to keep a supply on hand. This list itemizes the key points to be retained from each meeting, followed by spaces to be filled in as meetings are held.

Among the points you will want to have a clear record of are the following:

■ Date of meeting.
■ Length of meeting.
■ Origin of meeting (advert, motivating letter, personal contact, etc).
■ Name of company or executive search firm.
■ If with a company, its activity and size.
■ Name and title of person (or persons) seen.
■. Title and short description of post available (unless it is just a 'get-acquainted' meeting).
■ Salary offered.
■ To whom does the job report?
■ Your general impressions.
■ Next steps to take and when.

Always read over the notes you have made just before a second meeting — no matter how confident you are of your memory. Doing so will resensitize you to the feeling of the first meeting and boost your confidence that you have the needed facts at your disposal.

THE FOLLOW-UP LETTER

Few candidates bother to send a note after each meeting. This is all the more reason for doing so — but always in a way likely to reinforce your situation. The letter that simply says 'thanks for the meeting' is not likely to be helpful.

However, there is another way of proceeding. This is to produce a communication that nails down your discussion. The most direct way to do so results from your promise, made in the meeting, to send a CV. Such a covering letter can highlight any points you feel need to be stressed and should reiterate your enthusiasm (provided it exists) for the post discussed.

Another kind of letter is the one intended for people who have examined your CV already. This is often the case when your contact has been with an executive recruitment firm, many of which insist on such documentation. In preparing your letter, keep in mind that the recruiter is your ally if the meeting has gone well. He will very likely welcome any support from you in promoting your candidature and thus earning his fee. Accordingly, your might enclose with your letter documentation, such as copies of letters of commendation or certificates of award.

A business-like way to close a letter of thanks is to refer to any next step that might have been agreed on. Thus a typical final paragraph might well be: 'As you suggested during our talk, I look forward to hearing from you towards the end of this month as to the possibility of our meeting again.'

Important to avoid is any suggestion that your letter is written simply to convey a banal 'thank you'. (In reality, the other person might more realistically thank you for your presence as a possible solution to his or her recruiting problem.)

Need I add that any letter you send should be posted promptly? Names and faces can quickly detach themselves from the memory of an interviewer who is seeing many candidates. The least your letter can hope to accomplish is to reinforce your own identity in the interviewer's memory before time may erase it.

KEEPING IN CONTACT

What to do when the other person fails to get back in touch with you as promised? Phone his or her office to request a response? Dispatch a reminder letter? Either can seem to be a criticism of the individual, implying that he or she has not kept his or her word. This kind of exigence also may be interpreted — perhaps correctly — as a sign of anxiety or impatience.

Wait another day? Time passes. Without your knowledge another candidate may have been offered the post. (A repeated failure of executive recruiters is to keep applicants informed of developments, especially when they are negative.)

There is, nonetheless, one way to maintain contact without risk. Keep an eye on the contents of the business and/or technical publications you read (not the widely-distributed daily press). If your mind is so oriented, you are likely to come across an article of potential interest to the person with whom you have been in contact. Once you have identified such an item, send it to him or her. A short, handwritten accompanying note of transmittal is all that is necessary. Your message is simple: you saw the article and thought it might interest your contact.

It is well to skip such trite and obvious phrases as 'hoping to hear from you soon' or 'looking forward to our next meeting'. If your note fails to elicit even an acknowledgement, you can take the lack of response as confirmation that nothing is likely to come from this particular possibility.

Nearing the end of your search, you will have to decide which job offer to accept. But often a problem of timing can complicate matters. This happens when you are pressed to accept a post that is not as desirable as another for which you feel you have a good chance. Yet you do not want to let go of the 'bird in hand'. This is a critical moment but, as the next chapter shows, ways exist to deal with it.

12

Slowing Down, Speeding Up

What constitutes the ideal post? A checklist is not hard to create; such a position is likely to offer:

1. The kind of activity that meets your own particular needs if you are to have real satisfaction in the course of your working life.
2. A clear possibility of progression in terms of salary and status.
3. An agreeable environment (pleasant workplace, congenial colleagues, good geographical situation, the kind of product that appeals to you).
4. A correct salary.

To achieve a position that meets these criteria you are almost certainly going to have to have several concrete job offers in order to weigh and measure one against the other before making a choice. This, of course, is the reason for the important investment of time and energy proposed in this book.

However, there can be — and often is — a gap between theory and practice. In practice, specific job offers have an annoying way of failing to come along within a convenient time framework. In other words, a post in which you are only mildly interested materializes before you have received a concrete offer from your first choice.

In Chapter 2, I proposed a co-ordinated plan of market research intended to harvest your results within a limited span so as to make possible a real choice. Even within a 'reasonable period', however, examples of awkward timing are not unusual.

A real effort to find 'the right job' is a goal that is not entirely self-serving. After all, your own satisfaction is only one-half of the equation. The other half concerns the wellbeing of your ultimate employer. A well-managed enterprise is bound to make every effort to slot the right person into the right job. A candidate who would rather be working somewhere else is hardly likely to be the best possible choice. Regarded objectively, then, whatever efforts the candidate makes to end up within the right post are a boon to all.

Two kinds of 'adjustment' of timing may be needed to hold open a less favoured offer while awaiting a concrete offer from your No 1 choice. One kind of action is to slow down your decision on the former. The other is to speed up the arrival of a firm offer from your preferred choice. Here, then, are the ways you have at your disposal to slow down the hiring process.

SLOWING DOWN THE HIRING PROCESS

Step 1

Always remember that you are under no obligation to give an immediate answer to a concrete job offer, whether it reaches you by post, telephone or in person. Often companies feel an urgency to fill this or that post but even in this situation a future employer will recognize the right of the candidate to a period of reflection. If an organization fails to recognize this right, one can well question how serious is an employer who is prone to act in haste and to repent at leisure. Nearly always your appropriate initial response to an offer is to state your pleasure and your interest in the post but to add 'naturally I would like some time for reflection before giving you a definitive answer'. 'I understand' might well be the employer's response, 'but when may we hear from you?'. At this point I suggest you ask the question: 'When would you like to have my reply?' The answer will give you the extent of the first period of delay at your disposal.

Step 2

The time has now come when you must say 'yes' or 'no'. At this point your most useful response is to say 'yes in principle' but 'subject of course' to receiving a contract or letter of confirmation of the terms agreed on. The creation of this document plus the time of passage in the mail could result in a further delay of around one week.

Step 3

Once you have in hand the document you have requested you will find either omissions or a less-than-exact rendition of the terms arrived at in your discussions. Wait two or three days, then write a reply suggesting that the necessary changes be made. You will note here, I hope, my reliance on the written, rather than the spoken, word as a way to gain time. The result up to this point has been a total delay of 10 days to two weeks.

Step 4

Within 72 hours sign your contract and mail it off.

SPEEDING UP AN ORGANIZATION'S DECISION MAKING

To speed up the decision making of the preferred enterprise you will, of course, have been active in the opposite sense. The moment you have a verbal competing offer, you are justified in contacting immediately the firm that most interests you and with which you are in negotiation. Explain the reason you are under time pressure without, of course, naming the other company. State that you are being pushed to make a decision, but speak of your preference for the company of your interlocutor. Request a decision from him or her as soon as possible and ask when you might have a 'yes' or 'no'. Your application of the delaying tactics above can then be geared to this reply.

Breaking off negotiations

Even if you succeed in obtaining the contract you prefer there remains still the uncomfortable matter of breaking off negotiations with the first enterprise to request your services. You have, of course, accepted the post only 'in principle' but nonetheless you may feel some uneasiness about reversing your acceptance. I can only suggest to you that you might look at the affair from a broader perspective. No right-thinking company would wish to keep on its payroll a person who would rather be elsewhere — in other words to retain, because of a generalized sentiment of 'obligation', an undermotivated executive. By extension this same reasoning can apply to your handling of the receipt of a better job offer after you have actually signed a contract with another company. Personally, and, in a subjective sense, morally, you might find it hard to back out of your engagement. (Legally, at least, there is no problem about making such a reversal.) However, the fact remains that you will have caused considerable inconvenience to the company; your expressed regrets, in writing or in person, will not change that fact.

If you feel you need to steel yourself for such a situation, I suggest — and I believe with reason — that the company is far better equipped to cope with the problem than the individual. In the case of the company, we are speaking of an inconvenience; on the other hand the individual is dealing with a career choice that could well affect the remainder of the only life that is his or hers to live. In other words, 'charity begins at home'.

13

The Heart of the Matter

You are a 'marketable product'.

What does this mean? It has little to do with age — if your career progress has kept pace with the passage of time. Nor is your marketability necessarily linked to your education — provided that the results you have achieved in later life are noteworthy.

'Marketable?' Yes, but first and foremost you must make contact with potential buyers of your services.

Do words like 'sellers' and 'buyers' rub you up the wrong way? Then you would do well to reflect on what has happened to employer–employee relations since the Second World War. A few decades ago, a person setting forth on a career expected a lasting bond to exist between him or herself and his or her employer, with certain mutual obligations assumed by both.

Why this kind of reciprocal loyalty has all but disappeared is a matter for business sociologists and professors to elucidate. What is clear is that today most executives are required to — or elect to — change employers once or several times in the course of their career. Willingly or not, they become marketers of their own services.

The essential beginning of the process of constructive change is to open doors; most often by means of written communication. To get it right, ask yourself the following key questions.

KEY QUESTIONS IN THE PROCESS OF CONSTRUCTIVE CHANGE

Are you 'proactive' in your exploration of the job market?

Do not look for the word 'proactive' in your dictionary. It is an invented term because no other word seems quite to express the kind of initiative and originality I feel are so important in the matter of advancing one's self-interest. Certainly 'agressivity', with its bared-fangs connotation is not appropriate in this context. What I am referring to is the kind of activity that is the opposite of 'reactivity'. When we obey all of the rules and conventions generally considered to be 'correct' in a job search we are simply reacting to the dicta laid down by others. When we respond to advertisements by following in detail each minute instruction we also slide reactively into the faceless pool of job seekers. Industry wants and needs people of initiative and energy; your methods of presentation should reflect these qualities rather than simply those of a *bon enfant*. You understand, I am sure, that here I am not proposing bizarre, 'creative' approaches but rather that you simply present yourself on paper in the manner most advantageous to yourself.

Are you thinking in terms of sufficiently large numbers?

The statistics are there to prove the point that most candidates are overly conservative in the number of first approaches they make by mail. On average, one out of ten responses to help-wanted advertisements will produce a first meeting (not a job, or even a second meeting). Persons who make unsolicited mailings to executive search firms (those who do not advertise openings) seldom realize the limited number of searches any one cabinet is conducting at any one time — let us say five, six or seven — for a wide variety of executive profiles, perhaps — and only perhaps — including yours. Finally, there is the question of direct approaches to companies where a good score is to attain five meetings from 100 approaches. There exist, of course, other ways of making contact than these, such as getting in touch with friends and 'contacts'. However, I have already, I believe, made the point: to avoid disappointment, think big in terms of the number of your original contacts.

Are you seeking contacts — or asking for a job?

A good way to handicap your job-hunting campaign irreparably at the start is to solicit a job far and wide. By this I mean the kind of campaign that shoots out hundreds of CVs and form letters to a multitude of companies and recruiting firms proposing your services. I repeat my conviction that the CV is used far more often as a screening-out device than as a door into jobs. Make contact first by whatever means exist — motivating letters to companies, advice visit letters, chain letters to friends and contacts, 'third-party' letters to recruiters. After you have established a good human contact, your CV can follow and it is only at this point that you are entering into a candidature for a post. These remarks evidently do not apply to replies to help-wanted advertisements where you obviously are posing your candidature whether or not you submit your CV.

Are you doing your homework?

In setting words about yourself down on paper, regard yourself from outside your situation — as though you were a copywriter in an advertising agency fully aware of the substantial investment represented by the quality of your message. Indeed the investment at stake in your future career and the earnings it will produce is also considerable. Write with the other person in mind, using the word 'you' as often as possible. Use the present tense as often as you can; it is more immediate and interesting than the past. Do not lose sight of the affective content of each word; 'I am seeking' rather than 'I hope for', 'I propose' instead of 'I would be grateful for', 'My competences' rather than 'my experience'.

The same diligence and time that you devote to preparing documents will pay off equally in the matter of creating your mailing lists for the different types of communications we have discussed. In the cases of letters directly to companies always aim at the chief executive if only because his or her office is a traffic control centre for all kinds of incoming communications. But beware, the age of people in jobs of ultimate responsibility means that changes are frequent. Be sure that your sources of information are as current as possible; if there is doubt in the case of an enterprise particularly important to you, it is worth your while to telephone the head office to ask the name of the present incumbent. When writing out your lists I suggest that you use block letters to avoid possible secretarial errors in typing.

Are you following through?

Demanding as the creation of lists and letters may be, more work still remains to be done. This involves record-keeping, a matter easily overlooked. One reason is that most managers shy away from 'clerical details'. Another is that they risk becoming totally absorbed by the activity of making face-to-face contact. Yet only by maintaining a running tabulation of responses — positive, negative and 'maybe' — along with the dates received, can you measure your results and forecast when your campaign will be drawing to a close.

In addition, an *aide-mémoire* of the contents of each meeting is essential in preparing for second and third meetings with the same organization. You think you can recall, as time goes by, the details of every meeting? If so, you are a rare bird. Better play safe, and get the major points down on paper for reference when needed.

Posting a follow-up letter to each interviewer holding the key to an interesting post is a rarity. All the more reason that you should take advantage of this means to reinforce your contact.

AFTER CLOSURE

You have signed on for a new post. Your last chore remains: to inform people with whom you have had contact of your new situation. This is not merely a courtesy; in the case of executive search firms, you are paving the way for a future move, if and when indicated. Companies which have received you for one or more meetings should also be updated.

And that is it. Your starting date is set. Now is the time to take a vacation — minimum duration, two weeks. Wipe from your mind the stresses of your former post. Back off from the tensions and tribulations of your job search. In a word, enjoy a change and come back refreshed and in top form to take up your new challenge.

Does this imply that every activity connected with your 'self-marketing' should be tossed into the waste-paper basket? Not at all. I propose you keep all your records on hand until you are sure that your new situation is what you hoped it would be. This is only common sense. Typically, a 'honeymoon' period at the start of a new post can last six months or more.

You will know when all is well. That is the moment when you suddenly hear yourself saying to yourself, 'this job is fun'.

Appendix

To obtain the names of companies and people to contact, the following directories are likely to be the most useful. Since business directories tend to be costly, you are advised to address your librarian or trade organization for access.

Key British Enterprises. Gives data on the 20,000 most important companies in Great Britain. Published by Dun and Bradstreet.

The Personnel Manager's Yearbook. Not only lists prominent companies, with names to contact, but also contains a useful directory of recruitment agencies. Published by AP Information Services.

Kompass. An exhaustive international guide to major companies, particularly useful for its listing of organizations by geographical location. Published by Reed Information Services Ltd.

Who Owns Whom. A cross-referencing of interlocking holdings and affiliations. Published by Dun and Bradstreet.

The Executive Grapevine. A listing of names and addresses of recruitment agencies, particularly useful for its classification of agencies by the kinds of posts they seek to fill. Published by Executive Grapevine International.

The Times Top 1,000 Companies. Exactly what its name suggests. Contains data on size, product line, number of employees and chief operating officer. Published by Times Books.

Whitaker's Almanac. Useful if you need information on trade associations and unions, industrial research centres, the press, banks, etc. Published by J. Whitaker and Sons Ltd.

Handbook of Market Leaders. Who is on top, sector by sector. Published by Extel Financial Ltd.

Trade Associations and Professional Bodies of the UK. A listing. Published by Gale Research Ltd.

Directory of Executive Recruiters. An international guide. Published by Kennedy Publishing Co, Fitzwilliam, Maine, USA.

For information on foreign executive search companies, contact the commercial attaché of the embassy representing in Britain the country or countries that interest you. Some of these services, such as that of Australia, may offer further information on conditions and lists of companies.

Index